ANIMALS IN SOCIETY

Facts and Perspectives on our Treatment of Animals

WITHDRAWN

Zoe Weil

ANIMALEARN

i

Acknowledgements

I would like to acknowledge the following people for their generous help in completing this text: Valerie Applebaum, Jenny Baldwin, Edwin Barkdoll, Gene Bauston, James Clark, Melissa Feldman, Patty Finch, Robert Kimball, Dr. John McArdle, Brad Miller, Dr. Robert Sharpe, Bernard Unti and Laura Yanne, for their careful reading and constructive criticism of the book; Leesuh Allen for her patience, and Dawn Knapp and Digital Arts for their creative design.

Printed on recycled paper

For the animals

Photographic credits

American Anti-Vivisection Society
12 bottom, 70 top, 74, 75, 79, 80

American Society for the Prevention of Cruelty to Animals
15 top, 38, 39 bottom, 43

Ann Cottrell Free
85

Anti Bont Comité
46 middle

Brian Gunn
15 bottom, 16 bottom, 76, 77

Cynthia Branigan
17 bottom, 28

Paul Duckworth
cover

Farm Sanctuary
58 bottom, 59, 60, 62, 67

The Fund for Animals
32, 33, 47

Greenpeace
63 bottom, 90 top & bottom, 91, 92, 93

Hope Sawyer Buyukmihci
87

John Foster
22, 23

New England Anti-Vivisection Society
36, 37 top, 39 middle

People for the Ethical Treatment of Animals
16 top, 25 top, 34, 39 top, 40 top, middle, 46 top, 51, 52, 61, 63 top, 64, 70 bottom, 71, 72, 73, 78

Philadelphia Museum of Art — Painting by Edward Hicks
7

Progressive Animal Welfare Society
13 top, 14 top

World Society for the Protection of Animals
46 bottom, 84 bottom

Zoe Weil
1, 2, 12 top, 13 bottom, 17 top, 18, 25 bottom, 50, 58 top, 65, 66, 84 top, 90 middle, 95

CONTENTS

CHAPTER 1

Animals in Society: Differing Views

Throughout human history we people have had relationships with animals. Sometimes our relationships have been harmonious and loving; sometimes they have been confrontational or exploitive. Sometimes they have been magical. Today, many are exploring the relationships between people and animals, examining the bonds of love as well as questioning the exploitation of and cruelty towards animals. More and more people are becoming concerned about our society's treatment of animals.

While some people are questioning the worldview which condones humanity's use, and even abuse, of animals, others do not believe that humans ought to be concerned about how animals are treated. There are many reasons why some people think that humans may dominate, kill, exploit and control other animals. Some religious traditions teach that humans are above animals, or that humans have dominion over animals. Sometimes people think that humans are better than animals because we can read, write, build cities, do algebra and construct codes of ethics and morality.

There have been people throughout history, like the French philosopher René Descartes, who have argued that animals have no feelings, that they are machines like a computer or a calculator. Some people *still* believe that animals have no feelings. These people may think that kicking a dog is no worse than kicking a desk or a television set.

As humans have learned more about animals, however, most have come to realize that many animals have complex nervous systems and can feel pain and pleasure in much the same way that humans do. We have noticed that they also have psychological states like those of humans and can experience fear, excitement, loneliness, boredom, affection and curiosity.

Our increased understanding of animals has led us to establish laws to protect them. In the United States it is illegal for a person to beat his or her pet dog or cat, or to deprive a pet of food, water and proper housing. It is also illegal to make dogs fight one another. Many states even have laws requiring that schools teach children how to treat animals properly.

It is not only dogs and cats who have feelings, however. Many other animals have the capacity to feel pain such as those animals whom humans eat, hunt, wear or experiment on. We cannot ask animals if they are in pain, but we can determine that because they respond to injury by crying out, whimpering, and behaving in other ways similar to humans who are in pain, they too can suffer when they are hurt. Sometimes it is difficult to tell if an animal can suffer. Can worms and lobsters suffer pain? What about butterflies, beetles and other insects? What about single-celled creatures such as amoebae?

We do not always know where to draw lines of distinction. For example, when is someone considered tall? We may not know for certain exactly when we should call someone tall, but we do know that somebody who is seven feet in height is tall. Likewise, we know that many animals, such as all mammals and birds, can feel pain.

What does pain have to do with concern for animals? Growing numbers of people feel that whether or not animals can do algebra, or read, or build cities, or construct ethical values, their capacity to suffer pain requires that we consider their interests before hurting them. These people argue that babies and young children, mentally retarded persons, senile individuals, and others who cannot do algebra or construct moral systems retain the right not to be exploited or abused. Just as all people should be protected from exploitation regardless of their mental capacities, so should all animals who are capable of suffering.

While our society has established laws to protect pet animals from pain and abuse, there are many other animals that we use, such as cows, pigs, chickens, horses, monkeys, and frogs, among others, who have little or no legal protection.

Some people are working to change the ways in which our society treats animals. The people who work to protect animals from abuse and exploitation are concerned with animal welfare, animal liberation or animal rights.

People concerned with animal welfare believe that animals may be used by people to satisfy human desires as long as the animals are cared for properly and treated humanely. Those who believe in animal rights or animal liberation do not think that animals should be used to

2

satisfy human desires. They believe that animals have inherent value, that they do not exist to serve humans, and that their interests should be respected by people. These animal advocates think that discriminating on the basis of species is immoral, just as discriminating on the basis of gender, religion, color or class is immoral. They call discrimination on the basis of species "speciesism."

Speciesism

(spē'•shēz•iz'•əm), n.

1. A prejudice or attitude of bias toward the interests of members of one's own species and against those of members of other species.

2. A word used to describe the widespread discrimination that is practiced by homo sapiens against the other species.

Those who do not believe in animal protection may think that any use and abuse of animals is acceptable, whether for luxury items, entertainment, or to satisfy human appetites. While these people do not usually sanction cruelty to animals, they are rarely concerned with respecting the true interests of animals or with establishing more legal protection for animals. Some of these people believe that animals exist only to serve human beings, and they do not consider an animal's ability to feel pain a relevant consideration for granting rights or legal protection.

In this book you will learn about the many ways in which animals are used in our society. You will be challenged to examine your own beliefs about animals, and to decide how you feel animals should be used, or not used, by people. As you read this book, consider whether you find yourself in sympathy with an animal rights or an animal welfare perspective, or whether you do not believe in protecting animals' interests at all.

Questions and Projects

1. What is exploitation? Describe some of the ways in which people are or have been exploited. Describe some of the ways in which animals are or have been exploited by people.

2. What is a right? Who decides who has rights and who doesn't? What should be the criteria for establishing rights?

3. What is the difference between a dog and a cow, or a cat and a pig, or a parakeet and a chicken in terms of their ability to feel pain or have interests of their own? Why do you think that some animals are accorded protection by law, while others are not? Do you think this is right? Why or why not?

4. When reading novels or textbooks, examine the underlying attitudes towards animals.

CHAPTER 2

Animals in Religious Traditions

Human values develop and evolve in many ways. Our values when we are young may differ markedly from our values when we become older. A person whose primary interest is making money, for example, may suddenly be moved to help others due to an experience which challenges deeply held beliefs.

The beliefs of our nation, our parents, our teachers, and our friends all influence our personal values. Sometimes people do not even question the beliefs with which they were raised, assuming that what they have been taught is good and right.

The way we think about animals has a lot to do with the worth we assign to them. We live in a society that is concerned with the well-being of dogs and cats because most people think highly of dogs and cats, whereas we rarely care about the well-being of rats and mice because many people do not like rats and mice.

When philosophers, judges, religious thinkers and politicians develop laws or theories about what is good and bad, they usually try to define values in a consistent and rational way. It is not always easy to determine good from bad, or right from wrong, however. For example, we say that it is wrong to kill people, but we distinguish between premeditated murder, terrorism, crimes of passion, justified warfare and killing in self-defense. Thus, most, but not all killing is wrong. Our values change according to the circumstances. How we judge right from wrong depends on many factors: our self-interest, our fear of reprisal, our religious teachings, our society's standards, our own inner feelings, our ability to think rationally, and our compassion.

How do our values and beliefs come into play when we think about animals? A hunter may say that it is not wrong to kill an animal for sport; a wearer of fur coats may say that it is not wrong to kill an animal for fashion; a farmer may say that it is not wrong to kill an animal to satisfy our palates; a professional exterminator may say that it is not wrong to kill an animal perceived as a pest; a scientist may say that it is not wrong to kill an animal to help human health or increase knowledge; a perfume user may say that it is not wrong to kill an animal to ensure that a perfume is not harmful, and a poacher may say

5

that it is not wrong to kill an animal for money.

On the other hand, there are people who say that killing animals for any of these reasons is immoral. They believe that just as we do not kill people for food, sport, entertainment, or science, killing animals for these reasons is wrong.

Values in Religious Traditions

In different countries and communities one often finds different ethics and values. One way in which values are developed and moral codes are established is through religious traditions. Practically all religions teach us that killing is wrong, that we ought to be kind to our neighbors, and that we must care for the elderly and the ill. What do religious traditions teach us about our relationship with animals?

Judaism and Christianity

In the Jewish Bible, known as the Old Testament among Christians, God grants human beings "dominion" over the earth and all of the creatures who inhabit the earth. The meaning of dominion is open to interpretation, however. Some people have interpreted dominion to mean that, as humans, we have total power and control over the natural world and everything in it. According to this viewpoint, humans may do whatever we want to the earth and to animals. Others have interpreted the word dominion to mean that while we may have power to manipulate and even to dominate the earth, we are obligated to be its stewards, or caretakers, in much the same way that God is a caretaker of humans. Most Jewish rabbis and Christian theologians believe that humans are given dominion with the obligation to be caretakers.

There are many passages in the Bible in which humans are instructed to be kind to animals. We are advised to kill animals humanely, causing the least amount of pain, and we are instructed to give working animals time to rest just as humans are given time to relax. Animals are still used, however, still eaten and still worked in the fields to serve humans. Does this mean that Judaism and Christianity teach that animals are ours to use as we see fit?

A literal reading of the Bible does not always provide answers to contemporary questions. Theologians must interpret the scriptures for insight into the meaning and intention of the Bible. For example, the Bible offers instructions concerning the proper treatment of human slaves. Do these instructions indicate that slavery is acceptable? Jews and

Saint Francis speaks to birds. Many Christian saints have respected animals, Saint Francis being one of the most renowned.

Christians now believe that slavery is wrong even though it appears to be sanctioned in the Bible.

How, then, are we to interpret the Bible's teachings about animals? Much has changed since the Bible was written, and modern-day theologians must interpret the scriptures in order to evaluate our relationship with and our treatment of animals. Faced with the multitude of ways in which animals are used, and often abused, in contemporary society, some rabbis, ministers and priests now believe that much of what happens to animals in our culture is wrong. These religious leaders are working to make people more aware of the abuses animals suffer so that we may eat meat or use certain soaps or go to the circus. They feel strongly that God did not intend for animals to suffer to satisfy human desires.

Before the flood described in the Bible, the animals of the world are saved on Noah's Ark.

Not all Jewish and Christian leaders teach respect and compassion toward animals. There are many theologians who do not consider the well-being of animals to be an important concern for religious people. During the long histories of Judaism and Christianity, concern about animals and the environment has often been neglected. A growing number of religious thinkers, however, are now changing their attitudes, just as their predecessors changed their attitudes about slavery.

Other World Religions

Within certain religious traditions in the East, such as Buddhism and Hinduism, animals are viewed with great respect and are treated with compassion. Most Buddhists and many Hindus are vegetarians. They do not eat any animals because they believe that killing animals for food is wrong. The members of one Hindu sect, the Jains, practice compassion toward all beings in a very strict fashion. Not only are Jains vegetarians, many of them even brush the ground in front of their feet in order to avoid stepping on any insects or small creatures in their path.

Within Islam, the Prophet Muhammad's teachings include injunc-

7

The Hindu God Krishna with a cow. Cows are considered to be sacred in Hinduism.

tions about kindness toward animals. The Islamic holy book, the Koran, forbids animal fighting, mutilation of live animals, or the killing of animals without a justifiable reason. This last admonition raises a central question which anyone who considers our relationship to animals will face again and again. What does "justifiable" mean? Is it justifiable to kill animals for food when non-animal food is available? Is it justifiable to kill animals to ensure the safety of beauty items such as lipstick and cologne? Is it justifiable to kill animals for fun? Muslim leaders continue to interpret the Koran for answers to these questions.

Earth-Centered Traditions

There are many religious traditions which are not organized with churches, temples, synagogues, and mosques, or with leaders like priests, rabbis, ministers, or gurus. The native people of America, often called Indians, have their own religious traditions. In most tribes, respect for animals is of great importance. Animals are part of the sacred earth and are regarded with reverence. Native Americans often do eat animals and have used animal hides historically for clothing and shelter, but the hunting and slaughter of animals have been carried out with care and seriousness. It is unusual for a Native American to kill an animal for fun or sport. Traditionally, when Native Americans have killed for food they have offered prayers and thanks to the animal spirits.

All over the world, from Africa to Australia to South America to Eurasia, many native peoples treat animals with deep respect. The religious values of these aboriginal peoples often stress the divinity in all of nature.

Animal Sacrifice

In the ancient Jewish and Christian scriptures animal sacrifice is commonplace. Today, Jews and Christians have rejected animal sacrifice as cruel and unnecessary. There are still some religious groups which practice animal sacrifice, however. One well-known group is Santeria which is followed by many people in the Caribbean and some people in North America. While the leaders of Santeria argue that the

8

principle of religious freedom protects their right to sacrifice animals in their rituals, others assert that such sacrifice is inhumane and cannot be condoned. The United States has never interpreted freedom of religion to mean complete freedom of behavior. (If a religious sect wished to sacrifice human infants, our government would not allow such behavior.) Likewise, many people believe that animal sacrifice should be outlawed.

Conclusion

Religious traditions offer people a moral framework and guidelines for behavior. While some religions are inherently life-affirming and respectful of animals and the environment, others have a history of indifference toward animals and nature. Due to increased awareness of our global ecological crisis as well as the range of abuses which animals suffer, many religions are now focusing attention on the principle of respect for other life forms and the environment itself.

Questions and Projects

1. Is there a difference between killing animals for religious purposes and scientific or food purposes? Do you consider one "sacrifice" moral while another is immoral? Explain.
2. Hindus revere cows, so cows in India are protected from slaughter and consumption. Americans are especially fond of their pets, so dogs and cats are protected from slaughter and human consumption. You were asked to think about the difference between a dog and a cow in Chapter One. After reading this chapter, what do you think the difference between a dog and a cow is now?
3. How does one determine appropriate values or decide when something is right or wrong? Sometimes what we think is right is not what our neighbor thinks is right. How do we determine the criteria by which society judges right and wrong?
4. Jesus encouraged love and compassion. Do animals deserve love and compassion?
5. Many religious and philosophical teachers, such as Mohandas Gandhi, Annie Besant and Albert Schweitzer, lived by a philosophy of reverence for life. These thinkers also taught others to respect animals. Research teachers, philosophers or religious leaders who taught compassion for other life forms, and develop a list of their quotes or teachings on the subject of respect for all life.

CHAPTER 3

Companion Animals

Most people in the United States share their homes with animals. Dogs and cats have been domesticated from their wild cousins and now depend on humans for shelter, food, care, and companionship. Fish, birds, rabbits, rodents, snakes, amphibians, lizards, ferrets and monkeys are also found in people's homes. Many of these companion animals seem happy to live with people and are pampered, loved and receive the best in veterinary care. Unfortunately, others do not belong in peoples' homes, and some companion animals are mistreated, and suffer or die at human hands.

In this chapter we will examine some of the factors which contribute to the widespread suffering of companion animals, and we will explore the responsibilities involved in keeping such animals in the home.

Dogs and Cats

Dogs and cats are our most common animal companions. We love them, care for them and pamper them. We also have laws protecting them from cruelty. It is illegal for us to deny our dogs and cats food, water and shelter, or to treat them inhumanely. Thousands of dogs and cats are confiscated every year by police and animal control officers because their owners have neglected and mistreated them.

It is not illegal, however, to permit our dogs and cats to breed, even though breeding leads directly to the problem of animal overpopulation. Over ten million dogs and cats are destroyed every year in pounds, shelters, humane societies and SPCA's throughout the United States. Even more are hit by cars, or are poisoned, or die of starvation on the streets. The reason for this tragedy is very simple: there are not enough homes for all of the dogs and cats in the world.

What Causes Pet Overpopulation?

Pet overpopulation is the result of animals breeding beyond the capacity of a community to house and care for them. Pet overpopulation begins when a person chooses to purchase a pet. Although there are already millions of homeless animals in shelters who need to be adopted, many people choose to buy a specific breed of puppy or kitten from a pet store or breeder. Because there is a demand for puppies and kittens, stores and breeders supply them.

Unfortunately, the birth of new animals in a world which is already severely overpopulated means that there are other animals who will not find a home. The older, unwanted animals are then killed because there is no room for them. If people who wished to share their home with companion animals simply adopted dogs and cats from their local animal shelter and spayed and neutered them, pet overpopulation, and pet destruction in shelters and pounds, would decrease and eventually cease altogether.

Puppies and kittens grow into dogs and cats, and often, the same people who wanted the pets become angry that the dogs are not housebroken, or upset that the cats scratch the furniture or spray the walls. These people may then bring their pets to an animal shelter. Will these animals find another home? Usually, the answer is no.

Obviously, many people do keep their pets and never think about giving their animals to a shelter. These same people, however, may think that there is nothing wrong with allowing their pets to breed. Some people think that their animals should be allowed to have puppies or kittens. They may think that watching the miracle of birth is a valuable experience for their families.

What happens to the newborn animals? Often, people are unable to find homes for all of the new animals. The unwanted puppies or kittens are abandoned to fend for themselves or are delivered to the shelter where many are killed because no one wants to adopt them. Sometimes people give the extra animals to neighbors and friends, who may in turn let them breed, thus perpetuating the problem of pet overpopulation.

Some people buy expensive dogs or cats with impressive pedigrees. When they breed these animals they have no trouble selling the puppies or kittens to others. At first glance, it might appear that such behavior causes no harm, since homes are usually found for all the offspring. Whenever there is a surplus, however, any additions to that surplus add to the problem. Every time a dog or cat is born and sold, there is another dog or cat in a

Because people allow dogs to breed, we have a severe pet overpopulation problem.

shelter who does not get adopted.

Some people think that they can control the reproductive behavior of their pets by keeping them in enclosures. This is not always the case. Male dogs often escape from backyards and run off when nearby females are in heat, and females in heat are often found by males even behind fences.

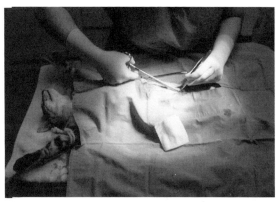

This cat is undergoing a spay operation to prevent pregnancy. Spay and neuter operations sterilize animals and are the most important protection against pet overpopulation.

How Can We Solve Pet Overpopulation?

The solution to the problem of pet overpopulation is very simple. We can stop allowing dogs and cats to reproduce at levels out of proportion to demand. If owners had their veterinarians sterilize all their dogs and cats through a simple spay or neuter operation the pet overpopulation problem would cease, and society would not have to kill so many unwanted animals. If those who want a pet would adopt an unwanted animal at the local shelter instead of going to a pet shop or breeder, the production of animals as a profit-making activity would diminish. Those people who are intent upon acquiring a purebred dog could also adopt one at the shelter, since 20–30% of the dogs in the nation's shelters and SPCA's are purebred.

We do not have to worry about running out of pets. At present, if 92% of all the dogs and cats in this country were sterilized, the remaining 8% could still provide all the animals people would ever want. There are many ways in which breeding could be regulated. Sterilization could be mandatory in those communities where pet overpopulation is a serious problem, and licenses for breeding could be acquired when the population stabilizes.

Some people regard pets as personal property and believe that owners should be able to do whatever they want with their animals,

including breed them. Others feel that the killing of millions of unwanted animals requires that some regulation of breeding must occur.

The cats in this barrel have been killed because there were no homes for them.

13

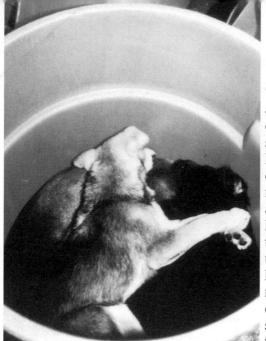

The dogs in this barrel have been killed because there are not enough homes for all the dogs in the United States.

Euthanasia

Euthanasia literally means "kind death." This term is often applied to animals who are destroyed in pounds, SPCA's, shelters and humane societies. Many shelter administrators employ the most humane methods available for killing animals, usually death by lethal injection. They believe that if we decide to kill unwanted animals, we must at least make sure that they do not suffer unduly during their deaths. Some humane societies, however, do not want to spend the extra money needed to ensure the most humane death, and so they continue to kill animals by gas or in decompression chambers. These methods of killing cause suffocation and can be very painful. Many states have passed laws to ensure that the animals destroyed in shelters are killed in the most humane way possible.

Since there are not enough homes for all the cats in America, this kitten may be killed.

Shelters

Animal shelters, SPCA's, humane societies and pounds house most of the unwanted animals which our society produces. They are places where animals wait to be adopted. They are also places where unwanted animals are killed. There are some people who think that animal shelters are terrible because animals are destroyed in them. While some humane societies, SPCA's and shelters are not as humane as others, it is ultimately the responsibility of all citizens to put an end to pet destruction in shelters. It is not the fault of shelters and humane societies that people buy animals from pet stores and breeders and then allow their pets to breed. Many shelters have programs to educate the public about pet overpopulation, but frequently people simply do not want to listen. They would rather buy a purebred puppy and allow the dog to have a litter than to take responsibility for the problem of pet overpopulation. These people may still consider the shelter a bad place, even though they themselves are contributing to the problem.

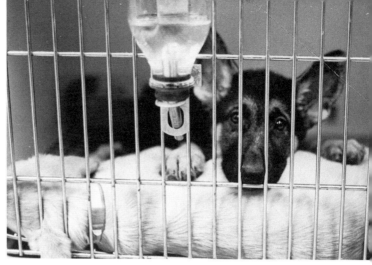

Awaiting adoption in an animal shelter, these dogs are likely to be killed if they are not adopted within a few days or weeks.

Puppy Mills

The puppies sold in pet stores often come from "puppy mills." As the name implies, puppy mills are places where dogs are bred continually to provide a steady supply of puppies for pet stores. Female dogs are kept in confinement and must reproduce constantly. Sometimes the animals remain in dirty cages for the duration of their lives, never receiving the love or kind touch of a human being. When they can no longer reproduce, they are killed.

Many pet shop owners acquire pets from these inhumane and unsanitary puppy mills with the belief that they are simply meeting the demand for certain animals. Some people have learned about the conditions in the puppy mills and have refused to buy pets or pet supplies from pet shops which sell puppy mill animals. When enough people stop purchasing pets from these pet shops perhaps profit loss will compel the store owners to reconsider their trade.

This dog is in a laboratory cage and will be utilized in experiments.

Pound Seizure

The term pound seizure applies to dogs and cats in pounds, shelters, SPCA's and humane societies who are "seized" for use by laboratories, medical and veterinary schools, biological supply houses and other institutions for

Cats like this are obtained from shelters for experimentation.

research, testing and educational purposes. Pound seizure laws differ from state to state. In some states the law forbids the release of pets to labs and medical institutions; in other states the law requires the release of unwanted animals to such institutions. There are also states in which the shelters or SPCA's may decide for themselves whether or not to provide animals for such purposes.

When dogs and cats are acquired for research, testing or education their fates are wholly uncertain. While some animals may die quickly, others may be used for long-term studies which cause considerable pain and suffering. Once the pound or shelter releases the animal to a research institution, the animal is rarely protected by anti-cruelty laws (see also Chapter Nine).

Animal experimenters often argue that the animals they acquire will be killed anyway, and so they might as well be used for human benefit. Opponents of pound seizure claim that the animals whom the researchers acquire are the same ones who are most adoptable: the friendly, docile and easily handled pets. They also point out that destruction at the shelter is quick and painless, while there are no guarantees that animals will be free from pain and suffering once they are in laboratories. Finally, opponents argue that pound seizure may violate a public trust that humane societies will provide shelter for animals and either a future with a new owner or a humane death. Citizens might be reluctant to bring a stray dog or cat to a shelter knowing that the animal might wind up in a painful experiment.

A dog used in a poisoning experiment.

Pet Theft

Pet owners need to be aware that unscrupulous animal dealers sometimes steal dogs and cats out of backyards, or answer "free to good home" advertisements, and then sell these same animals for research purposes. Because many laboratories, as well as medical and veterinary institutions, acquire animals from dealers without asking questions about their original source, there is a motive for dealer theft and deceit in acquiring dogs and cats for sale to researchers. Pet owners must be careful to protect their animals, and those who offer animals through newspaper advertisements should screen adoptors thoroughly (see Appendix C).

Birds sold on the street.

Birds

Birds are increasingly popular pets. Some of the birds kept in homes are born and raised in captivity; others are trapped in the wild and transported over long distances. Birds taken from their natural habitats suffer from trauma, starvation, confinement, and exposure. Four out of five die during capture, transportation or quarantine. Concerned individuals and organizations are trying to make the capture of wild birds for sale to consumers illegal, but because wild birds are a popular and profit-making item, there is strong resistance to protecting them. Some people will pay a great deal of money to own a scarlet macaw or Amazon parrot. Because many wild birds are slow to breed in captivity, more and more are being captured to satisfy the desires of consumers who want exotic birds.

Birds bred in captivity often suffer the same fate as dogs in puppy mills. Inadequate, unsanitary and crowded cages often lead to feather plucking and other neurotic behaviors. While some breeders are humane, many others perceive bird breeding simply as a business and do not give proper attention to the animals.

Bridled horses with bits in their mouths and blinders next to their eyes.

Birds sometimes suffer from neglect in people's homes. Initial delight in the new pet may give way to boredom and aggravation as the bird screeches in the early morning or makes a mess in the home. While some people love their birds and take good care of them, others do not realize that birds require a great deal of care, interest and attention.

Horses

Many people keep horses as companions and for horseback riding.

This leashed lion cub is someone's pet. Lions are wild animals, and do not belong in people's homes.

They feel that the horses enjoy being ridden as much as they enjoy riding them. Often the horses are treated very well, are provided with large grazing areas with other horses, and are loved by their owners. Some horses, however, live out their lives in small, isolated stalls and receive only occasional attention.

There are some people who believe that horses do not exist simply for human enjoyment. These people reject the keeping and training of horses for riding and entertainment. They also feel that horses kept in small stalls without contact with other horses are being treated inhumanely.

Exotic Pets

Exotic pets are those animals who have not been traditionally domesticated as companion animals. These can include monkeys, ferrets, snakes or other wild animals. The trade in exotic pets is rapidly increasing as more and more people find themselves desirous of an unusual animal. As with birds, capture and transportation take the lives of many animals. Captivity is also unsuitable for many species. Monkeys may bite, mess the house, and become overly protective; some ferrets will also bite as well as chew on telephone cords and electrical wires. When the owner discovers the difficulties in keeping an exotic pet, the animal may be confined in a small cage and suffer from loneliness and boredom.

Neglect and Abuse

Companion animals are too often neglected by their owners. Their water bowls may remain unfilled all day, cats' litter boxes may go for weeks unchanged, or dogs may be left alone for much too long a time. Many people who express great joy at the prospect of a new pet tire of their animal within a few weeks, and fail to give consistent love and care.

The abuse of animals by pet owners is also quite common. As with child abuse, animal abuse is often hidden behind closed doors. Dogs, cats, rabbits, horses and other companion animals are often the victims of an owner's anger or bad mood. Sometimes children who are mistreated by their parents in turn mistreat their own pets. Statistics show that there is a strong correlation between child abuse, animal abuse and other violent acts. A study conducted at Yale University revealed that many violent criminals have a history of animal abuse.

Often these same criminals were abused by their parents. This "cycle of abuse," as it is called, is difficult to stop.

Conclusion

Many people wish to share their homes with animals. They feel that their lives are enriched through relationships with other species, and believe that their well-treated animals enjoy the relationship as well.

Despite our love of pets, our desire for animal companions has resulted in tremendous animal suffering. We allow our dogs and cats to breed at such a rate that in the time it has taken you to read this chapter, approximately 1,000 dogs and cats have been born in the United States. Of these, about 800 will eventually die in shelters or on the streets because there are no homes for them.

Our desire for animal companions has also led to the destruction of millions of birds and other animals who are caught in the wild to become captive pets in people's homes.

We humans can and should examine our reasons for capturing wild animals, and for breeding our dogs and cats. We can also examine our motives for keeping animal companions to make sure that our desires are not inconsistent with the well-being of those with whom we would like to share our homes.

Questions and Projects

1. Why do you think laws protect dogs, cats, rabbits and guinea pigs in pet stores and in homes but do not protect them as fully when they are laboratory subjects?

2. Construct a model state law to deal with the problem of pet overpopulation.

3. What do you think can be done to stop the "cycle of abuse" described in this chapter?

4. A new species of animal is discovered, and your friend wants to acquire one as a pet. What should your friend consider before keeping the animal in captivity?

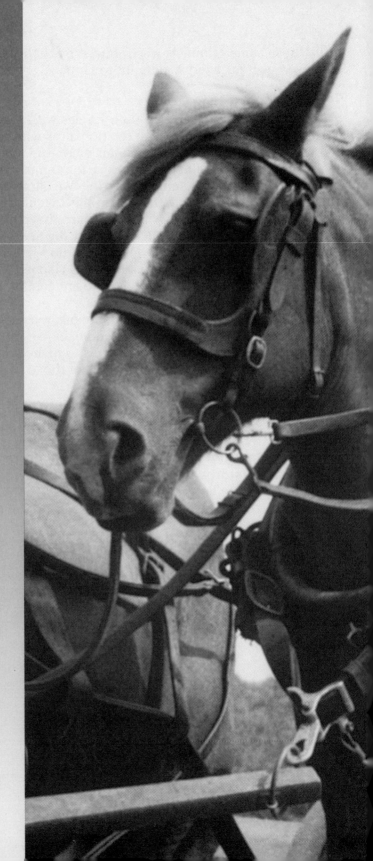

CHAPTER 4

Animals Serving Humans

Animals have been serving humans for thousands of years. Mules and horses have pulled ploughs, camels have carried travelers over miles of harsh terrain, and dogs have been protectors, shepherds, sled pullers and hunters. In addition to these traditional uses, in modern times, monkeys assist handicapped people, and marine mammals are used by the military.

Many people treat their animal servants very well. For instance, blind people with seeing-eye dogs are well-known for showing great care and kindness toward their animals. There are others, however, who do not treat their working animals humanely, and many a horse and mule has been beaten on the job.

Even if a working animal is well-treated, one may still ask whether it is fair, moral or right to use animals in the service of humans. Some people argue that no harm comes to working animals who are treated humanely, and that therefore nothing is wrong with utilizing them to serve humans. Others believe that animals have a right not to be domesticated and used by humans as servants or slaves.

This chapter examines a variety of circumstances in which animals are used to serve humans. In some instances there is little risk of animal suffering; in other instances there is a much greater risk. You are encouraged to consider how to draw lines of distinction between these different situations.

Dogs

People use dogs for a number of purposes. In this section we will consider some of the ways in which dogs serve human beings, leaving out "companionship" which was covered in Chapter Three.

Police Work

Dogs have been a great help in law enforcement. Their acute sense of smell enables them to find drugs and missing people far more easily than humans can. Their natural instinct to guard members of their pack, coupled with their lengthy training, often makes them exceptional protectors. Police officers who have dogs as partners are usually quite attached to their animals and treat them well.

Dogs must be trained to attack, however, and sometimes the training procedures are not humane. While most police departments employ humane and positive training techniques, there are some departments which acquire police dogs from trainers who use fear and intimidation to create an "attack dog." Dogs who have been trained through techniques of fear and intimidation are more likely to injure the wrong individual and wind up as uncontrollable animals who will have to be destroyed.

In the case of dogs who have been trained to discover drugs and other illegal substances, some ethical questions arise. Many of these animals are deprived of consistent play and affection in order to keep them focused fully on their "police work." Should humans deprive dogs of socialization and companionship so that the dogs can be better law enforcement aids?

Police dogs lead dangerous lives. Like their human partners they may be killed or injured in the line of duty. One of the differences between human and animal law enforcement agents, however, is that humans choose to become police officers whereas dogs are enlisted without their consent. Do humans have the right to train dogs for police work and force them to lead risky lives?

Police dogs perform a useful service for humans, and some people argue that their worth to humans justifies any ill-treatment or danger they may suffer in the process. Others feel that dogs are not slaves for humanity and should not have to risk danger or suffer inhumane treatment for human benefit. Some people feel that the best answer lies somewhere in between: dogs may be utilized by police officers as long as they are treated humanely and are not subjected to excessive dangers.

A police officer trains a dog to detect narcotics hidden inside a motorcycle.

Personal Protection

People often obtain dogs for personal protection, to guard a home or business. Since dogs naturally protect their territory and their pack (including their human pack), people do not really need special training techniques to create a dog protector. There are some individuals, however, who hire professional trainers, or who themselves attempt to train their dogs to be especially protective.

Although dogs will naturally protect their territory and their pack, the acquisition of a dog for the specific purpose of protection may not be humane. While some individuals assert that dogs need no more than food,

Dog detecting narcotics in a tool box.

water and shelter, most acknowledge that dogs need companionship and care above and beyond physical sustenance. These people believe that obtaining a dog for protection is only acceptable if the owner plans to provide a loving home for the animal. Protection can be one of the reasons for obtaining a dog, but it should not be the only one. It is worth noting that dogs who are loved are more likely to protect those who care for them than dogs who are given only food, water and lodging with no companionship or attention.

Dogs who undergo training to become especially protective are often mistreated. Some people will train their animals by using fear and intimidation to provoke vicious or hostile responses. Individuals who acquire dogs solely for protection, without concern for the dogs' welfare, are more likely to employ inhumane training than those who want loyal, loving companions who will, in addition, naturally protect the family.

Breeding for Profit

Some people purchase purebred animals in order to breed them for profit. While many of these people like dogs and enjoy their company, breeding the animals is a business venture. Some animals who are bred for profit are treated with love and care; others may be raised in puppy mill conditions (see Chapter Three).

Breeding may or may not be cruel to the individual animal required to reproduce, but it is practically always cruel in a larger sense. Because of pet overpopulation, millions of animals are destroyed in shelters and pounds every year, and millions more die of starvation, disease and injury on the streets. Any contribution to pet overpopulation, even if it consists of breeding purebreds, results in animal suffering and death. Whenever a puppy or kitten is born and sold, one more animal from the shelter has been denied a home. In addition, one need only visit an animal shelter to see the large numbers of purebred pets who have no homes (see also Chapter Three).

Some people feel that if their pet can generate a profit through breeding there is no harm done. The reality of pet overpopulation shows otherwise, but these people may feel that pet overpopulation is not their concern. They may view their animals simply as property, believing that if their property can become a source of income, there are no ethical concerns involved.

Hunting

Certain dogs are bred to assist in hunting. Many are trained by hunters to chase "game" and to retrieve dead animals. In the fox hunt, popularized by the British, beagles are trained to exhaust the fleeing fox through an elaborate chase.

While some people argue that the dogs enjoy helping hunters, others assert that the dogs are placed at great risk of injury. Dogs may be shot in the woods by hunters who mistake them for "game" animals or may become victims of leghold or other trapping devices (see also Chapter Five).

Animals Helping the Handicapped

Animals are sometimes used to help humans who have physical handicaps. Dogs help the blind by providing surrogate eyes, and they help the deaf by providing surrogate ears. Monkeys assist paralyzed individuals in performing household chores and tasks.

Most people with visual and auditory impairments treat their helper animals with love and kindness. These people depend on their dogs for their very lives. Most training centers also treat the dogs well, and train the animals humanely. Only occasionally does any abuse occur.

While many feel that there is no abuse involved in this particular form of animal use, others are concerned that the dogs may be denied opportunities to run and play and to be free from constant service to humans.

Compared with many of the other ways in which animals are used to serve humans, "seeing eye" and "hearing ear" service seem benign. The use of dogs for the blind and deaf is understandably more acceptable to many people than other uses of animals.

While there may be few problems with using dogs to help people with visual and hearing impairments, many problems arise when primates are used to assist people. Monkeys are utilized to help paralyzed people in performing household tasks, but monkeys are not as adapted to captivity as dogs. They are more difficult to train, can become overly protective of their owners, and have often bitten people. To avoid such problems, their sharp teeth are frequently removed, and they are usually trained with electric shocks.

Robotic alternatives to the use of monkeys exist and have been highly successful. They may be utilized at work or home and carry none of the risks associated with the use of monkeys. Other alternatives include human helpers and companions hired to assist those in need.

Some people believe that if the monkeys can be of service they should be used to help the handicapped. Others feel that the cruel training and the captivity of monkeys outweigh the benefits to their human owners. Since highly successful alternatives exist, they think that there is no reason for monkeys to be trained to assist paralyzed people.

Military Uses

Dogs, cats, monkeys, marine mammals and other animals are utilized by the military for service in warfare. Many of the animals are used in experiments to test weapons, radiation and chemicals for war (see Chapter Nine). Some are used for the placement and retrieval of explosives.

Monkey used in a United States military experiment.

During the Vietnam War dogs were used to help soldiers avoid land mines. Although the dogs saved many lives, the United States Army decided to leave the dogs in Vietnam after the war was over. Officials intended to abandon the dogs in a country where dog meat is a popular food.

Public outcry finally forced the Department of Defense to bring the dogs back to the United States, but the initial plan to abandon the dogs in Vietnam spoke clearly about the worth of the animals. The dogs were valuable as servants in wartime, but they were not respected in their own right. They were viewed as tools for the military like a

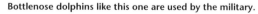

Bottlenose dolphins like this one are used by the military.

grenade or a tank, and nothing more.

Even if the dogs had been humanely trained and immediately placed in loving homes following the war, the ethical question of using dogs to fight our battles would still persist. The dogs risked their lives and often died. Although dogs are not considered citizens and do not hold the rights which humans hold, they were nonetheless drafted into service.

Marine mammals are also used by the military. Whales and dolphins are trained to locate explosives and other military devices in the ocean. They are also utilized as sentries and even as warriors protecting naval ships. Whales and dolphins used by the military are generally captured in the wild and kept in small pens. Capture, captivity and training are very stressful for these animals whose lifespans decrease markedly in captivity.

While some insist that the benefits derived from the use of animals in war outweigh any consideration of the animals' lives, others believe that animals should not be exploited for human warfare. They argue that it is humans who choose to go to war, not animals, and that therefore we should not utilize the natural abilities of animals to fight human battles.

Transportation, Labor and Agriculture

Animals have been used to aid in transportation, physical labor and

This deer was run over by a tractor when he was a fawn. His leg was amputated, and he will remain in an animal sanctuary because it is unlikely that he could survive in the wild.

This drawing by a Tibetan boy depicts the life of working elephants in India.

agriculture for thousands of years. While many cultures no longer rely heavily upon animals for these purposes, other societies still use animals to plow fields, provide transportation and lift great weights. For example, camels still carry nomads through the Sahara desert, and elephants still provide labor for logging in India.

In the United States, mules and horses have been replaced by trucks and cars. In some places however, mules still carry packs into wilderness areas, and people on horseback still round up farm animals on ranches. Certain religious practitioners, like the Amish, decline to use automobiles and depend on horses and mules for agricultural and transportation purposes.

While some people argue that harnesses and heavy plows take a toll on the horses and mules forced to pull, carry and transport, others feel that as long as the animals are treated well, there is no ethical dilemma in utilizing their strength and stamina for human gain.

One irony in the shift from animal to mechanical labor is the damage to the environment, to animal habitat and to individual animals caused by machines. Every year tractors run over fawns hidden in farmers' fields as well as displace rabbits, field mice and other animals. The pollution caused by tractors, trucks and other vehicles has also destroyed much animal habitat and threatens the survival of many animals on the planet. Some people claim that agricultural machinery has caused much more harm to animals than has ever occurred from utilizing animal servants for transportation and agriculture. Others argue that neither the use of polluting vehicles nor the use of animal servants is the answer. These people think that safer and more enlightened methods ought to be developed for assisting in agriculture.

Conclusion

Animals have served humans for millennia. We humans have relied on the instincts, strength and talents of animals to help transport us, sow our seeds, reap our fruits, fight our battles, and be our eyes, noses, ears and hands. During their service to humans some animals have been captured, beaten, shocked, whipped, and killed. Others have been loved, groomed, cared for, stroked and treated with kindness. While many agree that the mistreatment of animal servants is wrong, people often disagree about the criteria used to determine mistreatment or abuse. Is whipping a horse mistreatment? Is shocking a monkey mistreatment? Some people believe that whipping and shocking animals is abusive. Other people see no problem with these training or punishing techniques.

Horses worked on a farm.

Questions and Projects

1. What criteria should one use to determine whether a certain animal ought to be used to serve humans? Should kind treatment be the only criterion? Explain.

2. Construct a law to address issues surrounding the use of animal servants. Structure the law so that it covers three different kinds of animal use.

3. Write a list of ways in which animals serve humans that were not covered in this chapter. In each instance explain your view on the use of animals.

Another drawing by a Tibetan youth, this scene illustrates a working horse and oxen.

CHAPTER 5

Animals Used in Entertainment and Sport

Parents take their children to zoos, to rodeos, to sea parks and to circuses. Adults gamble at the racetracks. Some people fish and hunt. Animals are used in all of these forms of human entertainment. They are also often used in movies and television.

Whenever entertainment involves animal use it is important to examine whether the animals are treated humanely, and, when animals are killed or forced to perform unnatural acts, whether that entertainment is justified at all.

This chapter may make you uncomfortable. Most of us have enjoyed trips to the zoo or to the circus. Some of us have spent time with our families hunting or fishing. It is not easy to examine our behavior in light of new considerations, but for the animals' sake we should consider if we are exploiting and abusing animals for our own entertainment, and if so, whether such behavior is acceptable.

Killing for Pleasure

Hunting

When we speak about hunting we must distinguish between its several forms. An Inuit (also known as an Eskimo) who kills animals for survival is hunting for subsistence, whereas a person who lives in the suburbs and hunts or fishes is hunting for fun. The distinction is important. In one instance killing takes place for survival only; in the other, it takes place for enjoyment.

Some insist that hunting is a wildlife management tool and believe that people must hunt to control animal populations. They argue that hunting is an altruistic, or at least a mutually beneficial activity. Because natural predators like wolves and many of the large cats are now rare in the wild (they have been killed and displaced by people), humans, they assert, must take the place of these predators and thin the herds. Hunters also point out that nature can be quite cruel, and that animals who are killed by weapons suffer less than animals who die from natural causes.

Others point out, however, that state and federally owned lands are

A hunter drags his kill.

often artificially managed to increase the herds of animals and to cater to the interests of hunters. For example, deer like to eat the leaves of small bushes and scrub brushes. Instead of allowing trees to grow tall and thereby block the growth of brush, many state agencies will burn and raze the forests in order to create more brush for an environment congenial to greater numbers of deer. Those who object to sport hunting assert that many wildlife management departments maintain high levels of "game" animals in order to obtain greater profits from the fees which are paid by hunters for licenses to kill wildlife.

People who are opposed to sport hunting admit that nature can be harsh but disagree with hunters about the extent to which animals suffer in the wild. They do not believe that hunters really intend to relieve animal suffering when they go into the woods to shoot and kill wildlife.

In the wild, predators, harsh winters and other environmental factors cause the death of weak, old, and sick animals. This natural regulation preserves healthy and strong animals and keeps the numbers of animals in balance with the environment. Wildlife

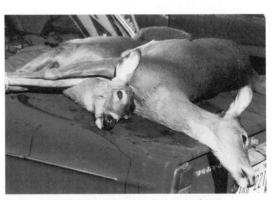
Dead deer strapped to the trunk of a car.

management agencies intervene in this natural system by continuing to allow hunters to kill predator animals such as bears, cats and coyotes. When the predators are killed, the prey animals increase. The hunters then claim that they must take the place of animal predators and kill the prey animals. Hunters rarely kill the weak, old and sick animals, however. Instead, hunters often shoot the biggest and strongest animals. During buck (male deer) season, hunters often aim for the bucks with the largest set of antlers. By killing the strong, healthy animals, hunters reduce the viability and health of the herd.

Even when predators do not exist, environmental influences still work to control the population of animals. For example, deer cannot reproduce indefinitely because the environment cannot sustain them. The size of a herd eventually adjusts to the available food supply. The reproductive behaviors of the animals also change according to environmental factors. For example, does may produce fewer offspring when food and space are scarce, and more when food and space are plentiful. Supporters of hunting argue, however, that significant fluctuations in herd size may occur, resulting in large numbers of deer dying of starvation one winter, followed by small numbers the next.

Whenever humans encroach on wild lands, animals are displaced. They have no option but to stray into what suddenly is termed human territory. Humans may then declare that the animals are a nuisance, decry their large numbers, and insist that hunting is not only essential for human interests but is also necessary to prevent the animals from dying of starvation. Hunting is seen by these people as both indispensable and benevolent.

Heads of dead animals are often displayed as trophies.

Others insist that establishing hunts is not benevolent and assert that the implementation of fencing, designated land for wildlife, and innovative chemical birth control methods would be more appropriate methods for eliminating the hazards associated with the growing population of a certain species. There are many researchers who think that birth control methods promise to be an effective and humane population control technique, particularly in urban and suburban areas.

In the case where killing is deemed essential, after all other options are exhausted, some who are generally opposed to hunting may support the employment of professional sharpshooters who will kill animals quickly and humanely, not for fun or sport.

There are some forms of hunting and shooting which make no pretense to manage wildlife:

Whole animals are stuffed for display.

–*Trophy Hunting:* Some individuals hunt for "trophies." They kill bears to obtain rugs for the living room or shoot bull elks for antler displays above the fireplace. Sometimes avid trophy hunters will even poach (kill animals illegally). There are many animals who are threatened with extinction because of poachers. Some trophy hunters will kill exotic wildlife at hunting ranches. These "hunters" pay a fee to the ranch for permission to kill animals.

–*Fox Hunting:* In Great Britain fox hunting remains a popular activity. Using dogs to chase foxes until the foxes are thoroughly exhausted,

Animal trapped in a steel-jaw leghold trap.

the hunters follow the chase on horseback and then kill the worn out foxes, or allow the dog pack to tear the foxes apart. The pain and suffering which the foxes endure is often masked by the glamor of the fancy red coats and upper class social customs of the fox hunters.

–Pigeon Shoots: Pigeon shoots are examples of wildlife slaughter which have been established as pure entertainment. Pigeons are either bred or captured and then transported in small boxes to the location of the pigeon shoot. When the boxes are opened the birds attempt to fly away to freedom. Their disorientation makes them easy targets, and the shooters gun them down immediately. It is often children who collect the dead and dying pigeons and kill the injured birds by wringing their necks. Because so many people feel that pigeon shoots are cruel and frivolous, they are illegal in most states, but in some areas pigeon shoots are still maintained as community events.

–Mourning Dove and Water Fowl Hunts: Millions of doves are killed every year for pleasure, and millions of ducks are shot despite the fact that duck populations are decreasing markedly. Decoys, human-made ponds and other environmental manipulations lure birds to hunting areas where they are killed. Lead bullets which sink to the bottom of ponds and lakes also poison thousands more ducks and geese who feed on contaminated food and lead shot.

–Bow and Arrow Hunts: As technology has developed, so has the hunters' arsenal of weapons. When hunted with guns animals have little chance of escape, but at least the guns do kill more quickly and more humanely than bows and arrows. Despite advances in weapons technology, some hunters prefer the less accurate but more challenging bow and arrow. When bows and arrows are used, 50% of the animals are crippled and wounded. They may escape the hunter but eventually die slowly and painfully from infection or blood loss.

Some trappers crush animals to death.

Trapping

There are some people who kill animals with traps rather than with guns. While trapping is rarely done for sport alone, it falls into the larger category of wildlife management and outdoor sport. One common trapping device, the steel-jaw leghold trap, clamps sharp steel teeth around an animal's limb. Trappers place the devices in forests, fields and even underwater, and bait them with food or animal scents. When an animal approaches the trap and steps on the trap's hidden metal pad, the sharp edges spring shut around the animal's leg. Leghold traps capture indiscriminately. A trap meant for a fox or raccoon may inadvertently capture an eagle, cat or dog.

While many trappers assert that the trapped animals do not suffer, veterinarians point out that the traps are quite painful. Fully conscious animals starve, become dehydrated and often bleed profusely until the trapper checks the trap and finishes the job of killing. Nocturnal animals also endure the terror of being trapped in the open when daylight comes. Although trappers are required to check their traps frequently, in remote areas, some animals may suffer for as long as a week until the trapper comes to check the trap. Some animals (particularly nursing mothers) have been known to gnaw off their own feet in order to escape the traps.

Fishing

Fishing is considered a great American pastime. Television commercials feature fishing trips as beautiful moments in family interaction and parent-child relationships. Whether or not the fish is caught, scaled and eaten is often irrelevant. Many people fish, not for food, but simply for enjoyment. The fun comes in catching the fish, and quite a number of people will catch a fish, pry out the hook, throw the fish back, and fish some more.

Anglers will often say that the fish do not feel pain, but scientists inform us that fish have nerve endings in their mouths and are likely to feel pain when the hook sinks in. They also cannot breathe when out of water. During the time when the fish are reeled in and allowed to die out of water, and even in cases when they are disengaged from the hooks and thrown back, they suffer suffocation or strained breathing. They may also suffer jaw damage and dislocation during the removal of the hook.

Zoos

Many children delight in visiting the zoo, a place where they can observe a multitude of animals. Most children have little interaction with wild animals outside of the confines of zoos. Perhaps in their daily lives they may see squirrels and songbirds, pigeons and deer, rabbits and rats, but the large felines, the great wolves, moose, elk, buffalos and eagles are far from view – except at the zoo.

When zoos were first established in this country, animals were trapped in the wild, many on other continents, and transported to the United States. To facilitate the capture of one young animal whole families were often killed. At the zoo the animals were placed in small cages, and curious people came to view them.

The population of wild animals in captivity has grown. Most zoo animals are now bred in captivity, and it is less common for zoo animals to be trapped in the wild. When institutions desire a new and more

A caged bear living in a zoo.

exotic animal not bred in captivity, however, they will still find ways to obtain them. Not long ago, administrators at the Shedd Aquarium in Chicago commissioned the capture of a beluga whale for their new marine mammal exhibit.

In many zoos, cage size and other accommodations have grown and improved. Some zoos now call themselves "wildlife parks" and have created environments in which the animals have larger, more natural habitats, while human visitors must remain in the confines of their cars or on designated paths.

Such improvements at major zoological parks have been welcomed by animal advocates. There are still roadside zoos, antiquated zoos and petting zoos, however, and at these facilities thousands of animals are often confined in tiny cages which bear no resemblance to natural habitats and which may be totally unsuitable in meeting the animals' psychological and physical needs. Animals in roadside or petting zoos may live in filthy conditions, suffer the taunts and jeers of spectators, and endure constant petting, grabbing and chasing.

Some zoos breed animals in order to attract visitors to their baby animal exhibits, even though the zoo administrators know that there will be no room for these animals once they grow up. Often these young animals are destroyed when they are no longer considered cute. Sometimes surplus zoo animals are sold to hunting ranches where trophy hunters pay large sums of money for the chance to kill exotic animals for personal displays. Zoo administrators may defend such practices by pointing out how expensive it is to house and feed so many animals. Drawing crowds for baby animal displays, even if it means killing the animals when they grow up, is justified as a means of raising money to meet general operating expenses.

Monkeys in a zoo.

In even the most respected zoos, animals have been beaten, clubbed and treated cruelly because they have not responded to their trainers' instructions. Some of these same zoos have separated animal families and have caused unnecessary stress to the animals through the practice of buying, selling and trading. Many animals also cannot adapt well to zoo life, even in exemplary zoological parks. For some, the stress of confinement persists even in large cages.

Some people claim that zoos offer a positive educational experience and are invaluable resources for teaching people about animal needs and behaviors. Others claim that zoos are more oriented toward entertainment than education, and that animal behavior cannot be properly studied or understood in unnatural, captive environments. Opponents of zoos also assert that zoos reinforce the notion that it is all right to capture and cage animals so that they may serve human needs and interests.

More and more people agree that zoos must be reformed, and that the trend toward larger and better animal parks for the current population of captive animals must continue. Some animal rights advocates believe that zoos are inherently immoral, and have made a case for the abolition of zoos. While they encourage reform, they are strongly committed to the end of keeping animals in captivity.

There are other people who point out that natural habitats are diminishing at an alarming pace. They assert that the only hope for saving many animal species is by preserving them in zoos. These people feel that it is necessary to continue breeding animals in order to prevent their extinction. While they may not support

This eagle's habitat is disappearing. He now spends his life behind bars.

the notion that animals ought to be display objects for humans, they realize that wildlife parks which are not open to public view may not generate enough funds to provide the necessary care for so many wild animals.

Pony Rides

Many zoos and traveling animal shows offer pony rides to children. The ponies may carry hundreds of children in one day and endure the stress of excessive handling, pulling and riding. Some ponies pull carts which are weighed down with more children than the ponies can easily withstand. Housing for these animals is often inadequate and inhumane.

Those who do not wish to contribute to the financial success of these activities do not participate in the rides.

Carriage Horses

Some horses are forced to carry carriages filled with human passengers through city streets. These horses are referred to as "carriage horses" and are generally found in cities which attract tourists. While a few cities have laws protecting carriage horses, many people think that the regulations are inadequate and the enforcement lax. Carriage horses carry passengers during extremes of heat and cold, during rush hour when motor traffic is at its peak, and on very hard surfaces which can injure their legs and hooves.

The horses are forced to breathe in the exhaust fumes from cars, trucks and buses, and to endure the honking of horns and the danger of reckless car drivers.

While some assert that carriage horses are both traditional and quaint and bring pleasure to tourists visiting new cities, others insist that tourists can just as easily enjoy their visits through walking tours which do not exploit animals.

Horses are forced to pull carriages in traffic on city streets.

Circuses, Rodeos and Bullfights

Practically all circuses and rodeos use animals to provide entertainment. Circus elephants balance on one foot or on their trunks, bears walk on balls, tigers jump through flaming hoops, calves are roped by the neck, and, dressed in human garb, monkeys act silly for laughs.

Calf roped in a rodeo.

The fun and laughs at circuses and rodeos often belie a cruel fate for many of the animal entertainers. When not performing, most circus animals are confined in small cages or transport vehicles where freedom of movement is severely limited. Animals are declawed, defanged, muzzled, chained and tranquilized to prevent injury to their human trainers. Some trainers have been known to use whips and electric prods in order to force the animals to perform for people.

In many rodeos, the calf roping event causes calves to suffer broken bones, bruises, torn ligaments, and pulled muscles. In wild horse and bull riding, normally docile bulls and horses are often subjected to electric prods, caustic ointments, sharp spurs, and bucking straps tied around their groins to incite them to abnormal "bronco" behavior. When the health of these animals deteriorates as a result of these extreme conditions, they are usually slaughtered.

Elephants performing at a traveling circus.

During bullfights, bulls are tormented, stabbed and killed in front of an expectant audience. They often suffer cruel treatment before and during this most brutal of animal shows. The horses used in bullfights may also suffer abusive treatment, and many are gored and disemboweled during the fights.

Other forms of animal entertainment include "boxing" kangaroos, "wrestling" bears and "diving" mules. In these spectacles, the animals

Tigers are trained to jump through a flaming hoop at the circus.

A bucking strap cinched around this horse's waist provokes "bucking" in a rodeo.

endure confinement, abusive training, and exploitation during the performance of very unnatural activities.

The rationale for all of these animal performances is human entertainment and human profit. Those who support rodeos argue that the animals are not mistreated, and that they provide much joy, laughter and fun for human audiences. Animal advocates argue that the use of animals as performers is by definition exploitive and abusive. In their view, forcing animals to perform, to live in small cages, to endure harsh training and, usually, to be destroyed after their usefulness wanes, is immoral.

Animal advocates also argue that many of these activities provide entertainment specifically directed toward children who are unconsciously taught that the exploitation of animals is acceptable and even enjoyable. This lesson may prevent compassion and kindness from taking root in young people.

Racing

Gambling takes many forms in our country. People bet on cards, on dice and on football games. They also bet on horses and dogs trained to race for human enjoyment and human profit. Horse and dog racing are big businesses which can bring in thousands of dollars for the owners of the animals and the owners of the racetracks.

This mule is falling into pool of water for a "mule diving" show.

While supporters argue that the animals like to run and are treated especially well since their usefulness depends on their ability to perform, detractors point out that many abuses occur in the pursuit of profits. Good health would certainly seem to be a necessary prerequisite for good performance, but maximizing profit sometimes entails abuse. Just as some dishonest human athletes take drugs to increase their stamina and performance, unscrupulous racehorse owners will sometimes feed drugs to their animals to enable them to run quickly, even when they have injuries. Young horses, whose bones have not yet reached maturity, are sometimes raced despite the fact that racing can harm them. Old horses whose performances begin to fail are often destroyed.

Racing dogs suffer similar fates, and most are either destroyed when their speed diminishes or are sold to laboratories for research. Greyhound dogs are often trained through the chasing and killing of rabbits, kittens and other small animals.

Even when racehorses and dogs are treated humanely, racing involves risks for the animals. Many horses and dogs fall, break bones and suffer other injuries during the course of their racing careers.

Animal Fighting

Cockfighting and dogfighting are illegal in most places, but animal fighting nevertheless occurs throughout the fifty states. While some states have strict penalties, others ignore this cruel form of entertainment. As with horse and dog racing the motive for animal fighting is money and entertainment.

In cockfighting, male chickens are forced to fight each other while humans bet on the winner. The roosters are fitted with sharp spurs on their legs to enable them to cause the most damage to their opponent.

Dog fighting depends on extremely harsh and cruel training. In order to create a dog "fit for the fight," the dog must be trained to be vicious and brutal. Kittens and rabbits are often purchased for the dog to attack in order to encourage "bloodlust."

Dogs are not naturally vicious. Fear, intimidation, and physical punishment are part of the process of creating a vicious animal. Certain breeding practices help to increase those traits which will provide for a more aggressive fight. Pitbull terriers have been bred for centuries to be more aggressive towards other dogs than most breeds and to have larger, more powerful jaws. They are called pitbulls because traditionally the dogs are thrown into a pit where they fight in front of a crowd of gambling spectators. Often the fight is to the death. Although pitbulls are not born vicious, they may be more readily trained for the fight than other dogs. A vicious pitbull is the work of a cruel "master," not the work of nature.

Television and Films

When we turn on the television or go to the movies we are likely to see animals on the screen. Sometimes the animals are well-treated dogs and cats or pet birds lavished with love and attention. Other times, they are wild animals trained harshly to become screen stars. One might see monkeys and chimpanzees dressed in diapers, or tigers on leashes. These animals are raised and trained for a certain kind of performance and are sometimes beaten, whipped and then discarded when their work is complete.

There are a few organizations which monitor the use of animal actors in television commercials and in movies, but even they cannot guarantee that training before the performance was humane, or that life following the performance will be protected and secure.

Not infrequently, animals are killed during films. Although American law forbids the killing of most animals in films, if the movies are filmed in other countries, American laws do not apply. Horses jump off cliffs, and animals are shot during hunting scenes or in war movies. It is difficult for the moviegoer to know whether the images on the screen represent reality, or whether they are carefully staged performances. It is also usually impossible for the audience to know whether training prior to the performance was brutal and cruel.

Those who support the use of animals as entertainers assert that animals sell products and attract the interest of viewers. These people believe that animal actors are valuable to the economy. Those who are critical of such use of animals believe that animals, particularly wild animals, should not be forced to endure the unavoidable problems of training and performing. They point out that human actors benefit monetarily from their advertisements on television and their movie appearances, whereas animal actors receive no benefits at all.

Conclusion

Animals entertain us. Whether they perform, race, pace in their cages, or die from a bullet, arrow or knife, many people take pleasure in the spectacle and support the industries which provide these entertainments. It is clear that animals suffer for our entertainment. The hunted, fished and forced-to-fight suffer by the very nature of the activities in which they are unconsenting participants. The circus, rodeo, racing and roadside zoo animals often suffer from confinement, boredom and harsh training. Some live in filthy cages and are denied interaction with others of their species, and some break their bones and suffer injury.

While many people urge their legislators to provide legal protection against such cruelties, every individual has the power to limit and even stop the use of animals for entertainment. People who do not want to contribute their money to the perpetuation of cruelty in entertainment can boycott circuses, rodeos, zoos, racetracks, sea parks and films which use animals in ways which are inhumane. They can also write letters to industry leaders and urge others to avoid such entertainments.

Animal advocates who believe that it is immoral to kill animals for pleasure, as well as those people who oppose hunting because they are denied opportunities to enjoy the woods lest they risk being shot by hunters, face a difficult challenge. Pro-hunting lobbying groups, such as the National Rifle Association, have considerable political power, and

42

working against their interests can be difficult. People who object to hunting can protest, write articles, and encourage fish and game departments to respect and represent the interests of non-hunters. Hunters comprise only a small fraction of the total human population, but they maintain a virtual monopoly on the management of wild lands.

The United States is one of the very few countries to permit the use of the leghold trap. Legislation continues to be introduced in Congress to ban this device, but its proponents face fierce opposition from those groups which work to keep trapping legal.

Chained elephants marching down Fifth Avenue in New York City.

Questions and Projects

1. What criteria should one use to determine whether a particular form of animal entertainment is acceptable?

2. Find out whether and how your local fish and game department represents the interests of non-hunters.

3. Evaluate a zoo using the guidelines provided in Appendix F.

4. Suggest some entertainment alternatives to circuses and rodeos which do not use animals. Do you think that these would be as enjoyable to you or your friends? Explain.

5. Investigate a local rodeo or circus to determine its quality of animal care and write a report for your school newspaper.

6. Write down a list of entertainments which use animals that were not discussed in this chapter. In each case, examine whether such entertainment is humane or inhumane.

CHAPTER 6

Animals Used for Luxury Items

Animals are often used to provide humans with items of luxury. Fur coats, ivory jewelry, reptile skin shoes and bags, animal skin rugs, and exotic animal trophies are all products which cater to certain people's vanity and desire for status symbols.* Millions of animals are killed, and many species are approaching extinction because of the demand for non-essential items of fashion.

Because many species are headed toward extinction due to poaching for luxury items, laws are being established to protect certain animals. Elephants, who are killed for their ivory tusks, and whales, who are killed for their oils, are protected by many laws. While these laws do not stop poaching, they do help to limit the numbers of animals killed. These laws also reflect public opposition to the killing of these animals.

Wild animal species which are not endangered are rarely protected from abuse or cruelty, even when the abuse is perpetrated in the name of vanity. As public attitudes change and more people become aware of the cruelties done in the name of unnecessary luxury items, the practice of animal exploitation for fashion should decline.

Fur Industry

Some people perceive fur coats as a sign of wealth, fashion and success. The coats are often very expensive and are made for people who are desirous of material status symbols. It is true that fur coats are warm, but there are many types of warm coats which are not produced by killing animals.

There are two methods for obtaining pelts for fur coats: trapping and ranching. Since trapping is described in Chapter Five, we will look specifically at ranching in this chapter.

The images which come to mind when one hears the word "ranch" belie the reality of the small, cramped and often dirty cages which house the minks, beavers, nutria, chinchillas, rabbits and many other animals who are bred for fur. While the fur industry argues that the animals must be treated well in order for their fur to be beautiful, opponents point out that food and water alone are enough to keep animals who have beautiful fur, bearing beautiful fur. Psychological well-being is not a prerequisite for beautiful fur, and since the intent of ranchers is to maximize profit, only the minimum biological requirements of the animals are met. The ranched animals live in unnatural, confined conditions for the dura-

*Some furs and skins are worn by aboriginal peoples, like the Inuits (Eskimos), who do so out of necessity, not for fashion's sake.

tion of their lives. The method of killing is either suffocation, anal electrocution, or the breaking of the animal's neck. The most humane method, lethal injection, is eschewed because of the extra cost involved.

The fur industry, and fur wearers, assert that there is nothing wrong with using animals to keep warm in winter, or even in wearing animal fur to satisfy a desire to be fashionable. They believe that humans have every right to raise and kill animals for the sake of beauty and luxury. Others argue that this exploitation and cruelty in the name of fashion is immoral.

Many animals were killed for this fur jacket

Jewelry and Accessories

People adorn themselves in beautiful objects, from necklaces and earrings to hair clips and fancy shoes. Throughout history many of these objects have been made from parts of animals. The tusks of elephants and walruses have been carved into sculptures, bracelets and other objects. Reptiles such as alligators and snakes continue to be slaughtered for boot leather and purses. Tortoises are killed, and

Foxes on a fur "ranch" in the Netherlands.

their shells are carved into hair clips. Coral is taken from the sea for beads, and oysters are farmed for pearls.

While many non-animal objects may be substituted for ivory, pearls, coral and tortoise shell, those who are willing to pay the price, and those who are indifferent to the plight of the animals and their environment, often continue to purchase the animal products. Although it is now illegal to kill many animals because they are in danger of becoming extinct, poaching still continues because there exists a demand for animal products such as ivory.

In the case of ivory, unless owning, purchasing and trading this product becomes illegal, poachers will find a

Mink on a fur "ranch."

market. Many people are working to make trade in ivory and other animal products illegal in order to more effectively protect animals and the environment.

Conclusion

While some argue that humans have a right to kill animals for luxury items, others insist that killing is not justified for the frivolous reason of satisfying desires for beautiful objects.

Many people who are upset with the fur industry have attempted to effect change through various means. By calling attention to the cruelties in the industry, animal advocates are making the public aware that animal suffering is condoned and supported whenever someone wears

Reptile skin moccasins for sale.

fur. In many places fur wearing is becoming unfashionable. In Western Europe, for example, the fur industry has suffered great economic losses because the wearing of fur is considered to be shameful and unpopular.

In the United States, the fur industry has launched a campaign to discredit animal advocates. Furriers have put billboards up on streets and highways saying "America means freedom to wear fur." Many Americans, however, do not feel that their freedoms include the freedom to trap, cage and slaughter animals for the sake of fashion.

Questions and Projects

1. Why do you think that the American fur industry has used the notion of "freedom" to defend fur coats? When abolitionists sought to make slavery illegal, slave owners argued that they should have the freedom to own slaves. Do you think these are comparable situations? What are some freedoms which Americans are denied because of moral or ethical considerations?

2. What animals, not mentioned in this chapter, are used for jewelry or fashion?

3. Tactics to eliminate furs range from billboard advertisements, to approaching fur wearers with information pamphlets, to picketing furriers, to vandalizing stores. What tactics do you find acceptable? Which do you find unacceptable? Explain.

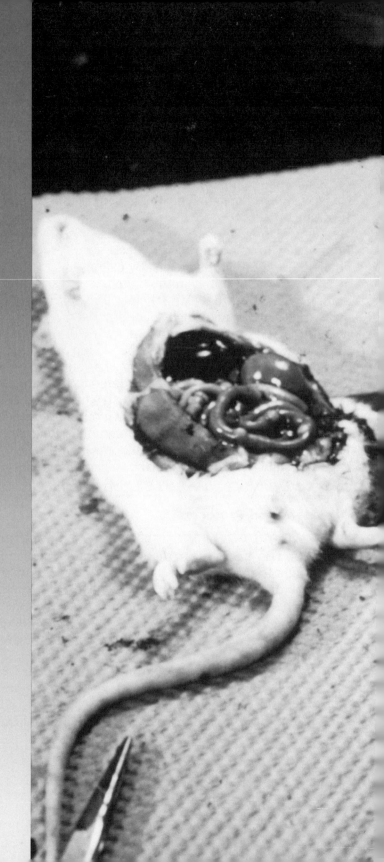

CHAPTER 7

Animals Used in Education

Animals are used in education from pre-school to graduate school. Whether as classroom pets or surgical subjects, animals are often viewed as tools for instruction. This chapter will examine the variety of ways in which animals are used to teach students and will consider both the morality and the merit of animal use in education.

Classroom Pets

It is rare that a child passes through the school system without encountering a classroom pet. Gerbils, hamsters, birds, fish, rabbits, guinea pigs, lizards, turtles and other small animals are common members of elementary and secondary school classrooms. These animals are obtained to teach lessons about animal behavior and habitat, or to teach compassion and responsible care for animals.

Such lessons are often successful. Committed teachers can and do demonstrate proper pet care, encourage their students to respect the animals' needs and psychological states, and provide for consistent home care during weekends and vacations.

Many times, however, the lessons backfire: nocturnal creatures such as hamsters and mice must endure the loud noises of the classroom and the unintentional distress caused by student interest in the middle of the day; fish are overfed by eager students and die quickly; cages are too small; the flight of birds is restricted; temperature changes in the school building cause stress to the animals; natural socialization is inhibited, or breeding produces unwanted offspring. The problems are manifold, and while they can be avoided by the careful selection of an appropriate animal and proper attention to the animal's well-being, accidents happen frequently, and the lessons of compassion and care can be completely undermined.

When a fish dies from overfeeding, or a hamster bites due to stress and fear, or a rabbit is abandoned at an animal shelter because no one wants to provide for the rabbit during the summer months, a powerful message is sent to the students: the animals' lives are not important, their care is not paramount, they exist for human benefit and enjoyment. No teacher intends to teach irresponsibility, but by keeping pets in the classroom teachers may unwittingly foster dispassionate attitudes among their students.

Teaching Biology

Biology is the study of living organisms, but in teaching biology most instructors and most curricula demand death, and often the suffering of animals as well.

Chick Hatching

Chick hatching is a common activity among elementary school classes. Fertile eggs are purchased, incubated and hatched in class. Students observe the miracle of birth and express delight and wonder at the sight of the newborn chicks.

Guinea pigs are often kept as classroom pets.

Such lessons naturally encourage a sense of awe at the life process. A classroom, however, is no place for a dozen growing chickens. Shortly after they are hatched the chicks are sent to chicken farms. The students are rarely told what fate will befall the birds.

Usually, the chickens are donated to the nearest farm which will take them. While some of the animals may live the remainder of their lives outdoors, with beaks intact and free to peck the ground, others will be penned up in crowded coops. Their beaks will be cut off, and they will be slaughtered as soon as they are large enough. The slaughtering process may take place at a commercial slaughterhouse, necessitating transport and resulting in stressful slaughter practices (see Chapter Eight).

Although rabbits are often kept in classrooms, they are difficult pets to keep in school. They need more exercise and space than can be provided in a classroom.

While children undoubtedly enjoy and learn from the experience of chick hatching, the chickens' lives are not free from abuse. Invariably,

50

the chickens become dinner for people. While teaching the miracle of life, the exercise implicitly teaches that the chickens' lives are expendable.

Some argue that a positive experience for the students outweighs the uncertain fate of the chickens, but others believe that unless the chickens will live out their lives free from exploitation, the miracle of life is only half the picture. Would the same teachers be willing to take their classes to a factory farming unit or slaughterhouse to round out the lesson about the life cycle of chickens?

Dissection of animals is common in biology education.

Dissection

Dissection is a part of most secondary school biology classes, although its use is declining nationally. Dissection may occur on worms and on cats, on previously killed and preserved fetal pigs or on frogs freshly pithed* in the classroom. The goal of dissection is to teach anatomy and physiology.

When preserved animals are used, neither students nor teachers know for certain how the animals were raised or killed. One commonly dissected animal, the mink, comes from a fur farm where the animals are raised in intensive confinement, in crowded metal mesh cages. They are killed by suffocation, electrocution or by having their necks broken.

Plastic models of frogs replace frog dissection in many schools.

Other animals used for dissection, such as cats, may also suffer abuse during rearing, caging, transporting and killing. Biological supply companies, which supply most of the animals used in dissection, normally utilize the least expensive techniques for housing and killing the animals. These are rarely the most humane procedures.

Many live animals, such as frogs, suffer capture and transportation, first to the biological supply company and then to the school, before they are killed in the classroom.

Once killed, the animals are dissected, their organs examined, and the details of the experience recorded by the student. Students have an opportunity to see and feel the actual organs of another species in

* Pithing refers to the procedure whereby frogs are killed by the insertion of a small, metal rod which severs their spinal cord.

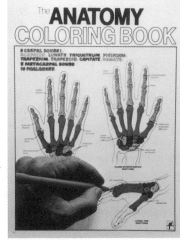

Plastic models like this one, of an earthworm, provide alternatives to animal dissection.

order to augment their understanding of anatomy and biological systems.

Teachers who utilize dissection as an educational device usually assert that the hands-on experience of opening up and observing the organs of a once-living organism is an invaluable educational experience, one that cannot be approached through models or other alternative means. Those who oppose dissection, however, point out that elaborate plastic models and computer programs not only demonstrate anatomical features, but are also more successful at teaching anatomy because they allow the student to repeat an exercise until the information is learned (see Appendix E).

Opponents of dissection assert further that dissection desensitizes students to life and instills indifference towards animals. When the dissection involves animals usually thought of as pets, such as cats, the procedure can be particularly distressing and psychologically harmful. Those opposed to dissection also point out the irony posed by dissection, arguing that one need not kill in order to learn about life.

Many students object to dissection requirements because dissection violates their ethical or religious beliefs. Often, schools will acknowledge a student's right to choose alternatives to dissection, but some educational institutions still insist that students participate even if they are morally opposed to the practice. When necessary, students are taking their objections to court to fight for their constitutional right to refuse to dissect animals.

Graduate School

The training of medical and veterinary school students often involves cutting open live animals. A common training procedure in many medical schools is the dog lab, in which live dogs are used to teach surgical techniques. The dogs are anesthetized while students practice surgery on their bodies. If they can be utilized for additional study, the dogs are allowed to recover to await further surgery. When their usefulness diminishes, they are killed.

The Anatomy Coloring Book allows students to learn anatomy without dissecting animals.

More and more students are objecting to the use of animals to teach surgical techniques, and all but a few medical schools allow students to utilize non-animal methods. There are some instructors who insist on live animal dissection, however. These professors believe that only by practicing surgical techniques on animals can the students become competent doctors.

Opponents of vivisection (live dissection) for medical students argue that students in other countries, such as England, pursue their medical training without vivisection and with no loss of surgical expertise. They also point out that practicing surgical techniques on nonhuman animals does not provide relevant learning experiences for performing surgery on humans. They assert that careful apprenticeship and tutelage under an experienced surgeon is more effective, more humane, and more conducive to learning. Another option for students who are set on careers requiring microsurgical skills is to practice on placental tissue, which is normally discarded after childbirth (see Appendix A).

For veterinary studies, one suggested alternative to the use of live, healthy animals is the use of animals who are scheduled to be euthanized due to disease, untreatable pain, or old age, and whose owners agree to one-time surgical practice provided that the animals are killed before waking up from anesthesia. Veterinary students may also learn surgical techniques under the supervision of experienced veterinarians.

While some students have been permitted to replace live animal labs with various alternatives, other students who have objected to live dissection have encountered significant resistance from medical and veterinary school administrators.

Zoos

Zoos are often justified on the basis of their educational value (see also Chapter Five). Since observing animals in the wild is becoming a rare experience for most people, one of the only opportunities for observing a variety of wild animals is in zoos.

The educational value of zoos is hotly debated, however. While some people insist that zoos provide a good opportunity for witnessing animal behavior, others point out that most zoos make little effort to provide a natural habitat for the animals, and that the behavior of animals in zoos does not represent their natural behavior.

Those critical of zoos also insist that the negative moral message outweighs the positive educational experience. Implicit in the philosophy of zoo education is the assumption that the capture, breeding and caging of wild animals is acceptable. This lesson may counteract the positive goal of wildlife appreciation.

Documentaries

Documentaries of animals in their natural habitats often provide an excellent educational experience for viewers. Normally, the scientists and naturalists who supervise the documentaries take great care to ensure the safety and well-being of the animals whose lives they are documenting.

Some directors, however, are more concerned with filming the perfect scene than with protecting the animals involved, and sometimes animals are injured or stressed during the production of the film. Some producers also stage scenes in order to film the chasing and killing of prey animals by predators. It is often difficult for the viewer to discern whether scenes have been staged, or whether the animals have been mistreated during production.

Films and documentaries can be of great educational value, but animal advocates insist that the safety and well-being of the animal subjects must be ensured.

Conclusion

What may be educationally valuable in one sense may be damaging in another. For example, what one learns about anatomy through dissection must be balanced with the implicit message that the dissected animal's life is expendable.

Other methods for teaching responsible pet care, anatomy, surgical techniques and animal behavior exist which do not cause stress, pain, or death to animals. While some believe that the benefits of using animals in education justify the death and potential suffering of animals, others insist that only humane means should be utilized. (See Appendix E).

Those students who find themselves in opposition to dissection or other uses of animals in education may demand the right not to participate in classes which violate their moral or religious beliefs. Although some students have had to fight for their right not to dissect in court, a growing number of schools do honor a student's right to pursue alternative lessons.

Questions and Projects

1. There are many alternatives to the keeping of classroom pets which teach about animal behavior and responsible pet care. Constructing a bird feeder outside the classroom window is an excellent project. Students may observe the birds in their own environment while still learning responsibility and compassion through the consistent replenishing of food throughout the winter. Write down some other possible alternatives to the keeping of classroom pets.

2. Train yourself to observe with care and attention by watching a documentary about animals with a critical eye and a pad and pencil in hand. Write down any questions and concerns which you have as you watch the program. Where is the camera crew? Do the animals seem startled when they face the camera? Do attacks and kills appear natural or contrived? Do the animals attempt to avoid the camera crew?

3. Go to a park or forest and sit quietly for an hour. Observe the animals nearby, noting their actions and behaviors. Repeat this exercise during the different seasons throughout the year and record your observations.

CHAPTER 8

Animals Used for Food and Clothing

It has been said that Americans love animals... for breakfast, lunch and dinner. Over five billion animals are raised and slaughtered for food every year in the United States. Most people eat meat and wear leather and wool, rarely considering the lives of the animals who feed and clothe them.

The days of Old McDonald's farm are over, replaced with the modern intensive farming industries catering to a new McDonalds. Most cows, pigs, chickens and turkeys no longer roam the barnyard, roll in the dirt, graze or peck on the ground. The majority of farm animals are now confined in crates, cages or in overcrowded buildings where they live out their lives as meat machines. Because farm animals have become cogs in the machinery of food production, people have coined the term "factory farm" to describe the modern intensive farming unit.

The scant legal protection accorded farm animals does not protect them from overcrowding, physical mutilations, social deprivation, excessive drug treatments or cruelty in the course of rearing, transportation and even slaughtering.

At its current scale animal agriculture is also contributing to environmental degradation through topsoil depletion, groundwater and air pollution, water waste, excessive use of fossil fuels, and deforestation (see also Chapter Twelve and Appendix B).

Physicians and nutritionists are discovering that the American meat-centered diet is not at all healthy. The high fat, protein and cholesterol content of animal products contributes to heart disease, strokes and cancer, as well as to other diseases (see Appendix B).

Many people who learn about the cruelties perpetrated on animals in factory farms decide to adopt a vegetarian diet. Not only do they enjoy the benefits of vegetarianism, the animals and the environment benefit as well.

Modern Meat Production

Poultry

Chickens are raised for two products: meat and eggs. The practice of intensive confinement farming is almost universal in the poultry industry. Over 90% of chicken meat and eggs are produced in factory farms.

Shortly after broiler chickens are hatched, their beaks are cut back with a hot blade. This process is called debeaking. While some say that

Meat is the flesh of slaughtered animals.

debeaking is painless, many veterinarians insist that the birds, who have sensitive nerve endings in their beaks, and who bleed during the procedure, suffer pain. The purpose of debeaking is to prevent cannibalistic behavior common among chickens who are raised in overcrowded conditions. Many factory farmers also trim the toes, not simply the toe nails, of the chickens.

Broiler chickens are placed in crowded, windowless buildings, where they are fattened for slaughter for approximately eight weeks. When the animals are full-sized they are transported by truck in small, crowded crates to slaughterhouses. Once in a slaughterhouse, the fully conscious chickens are hung upside down by their feet while they travel along a conveyor belt until they are stunned by an electrified liquid solution. Their necks are then cut, and they are placed in boiling water. Due to the huge numbers of chickens who undergo this process, the system sometimes fails to function properly. The result is that some conscious chickens are scalded in boiling water.

Because of overcrowding in factory farms, disease among the chickens is common. The chickens are fed a diet laced with drugs and antibiotics in order to prevent premature death due to disease. Most member nations of the European Economic Community have banned the routine, sub-therapeutic use of drugs and antibiotics in animal feed. They have done so because of their concern that when medically useful antibiotics are used in this way, bacteria can become resistant to their influence. These same antibiotics are then ineffective when used to combat human illness directly.

The United States has not followed the European trend, and instead supports the use of antibiotics as well as the continuing conditions which necessitate their use. (For more information regarding antibiotics in animal feed, see Appendix B.)

Readers should be aware that turkeys are raised in similar conditions to broiler chickens.

Unwanted male chicks are thrown away at a hatchery for layer hens.

Egg-laying hens face even more stressful conditions than broiler chickens. Because only female chickens are needed for egg laying facilities, the male chicks are killed immediately. Sometimes the male chicks are gassed; other times they are simply thrown into grinding machines while they are still alive, to become animal feed, or are tossed into a garbage bag where they are crushed by other chicks and suffocated.

Hens in battery cages in a typical factory farm.

Like the broiler chickens, the female chicks are debeaked to prevent feather plucking. They are placed in tiny cages, called battery cages, usually with four or five chickens in a space only a little bigger than a record album cover. Under these conditions the hens can barely move and cannot stretch their wings. They must stand on slanted, wire mesh for one to two years. Normally, chickens scratch on the ground looking for food. During the process of scratching, their claws are worn down and kept trim. In the wire cages the hens' claws sometimes grow so long that they curl around the wires and back into the animals' feet.

Although chickens would naturally live up to ten years, in intensive egg laying production they are killed after one or two years, when their productivity decreases. During the course of those several years, however, more than 10% die of disease, inability to get to food and water, or cannibalism due to overcrowding. Because thousands of hens are crowded into one building where environmental conditions are artificially manipulated to maximize egg laying, the level of production is high. The 10% loss does not affect the egg industry's profits significantly, so no efforts are made to ease crowding or to better the conditions for the chickens.

Animal advocates argue that the circumstances under which chickens and turkeys are raised are cruel. They point out that the same conditions, if applied to pet birds, are illegal. The poultry industry responds that the animals are in well-controlled facilities, that their food and water needs are always met, that the chickens are protected from predators and extremes of heat and cold, and that disease is prevented through drug treatment. The industry rarely admits, however, that the conditions in the factory farm facilities actually lead to the diseases which require drug-laced feed.

The Dairy and Veal Industries

Human beings are the only animals who drink milk after weaning. We are also the only animals (with the exception of domesticated dogs and

Most dairy cows are milked by machine.

cats) to drink the milk of another species. In order to obtain milk, female cows are repeatedly impregnated. When they give birth, their calves are quickly removed, and the milk meant for the calves is instead taken for human consumption.

Milking machines have replaced human hands. Cows' teats are hooked up to tubes which collect their milk. While some dairy cows spend time grazing when they are not being milked, others are confined for long stretches of time in crowded sheds. Because the dairy industry seeks the maximum quantity of milk from each animal, drugs and hormones are often administered to dairy cows to increase their milk production. Cows are also bred to be more effective milk producers. As a result of hormone treatments and breeding, many cows suffer from swollen and often diseased udders.

Cows, like human beings, are mammals. When their young are taken away from them at one or two days of age, the cows often exhibit signs of distress at the separation. Cows may bellow and cry out for days after their young are removed.

Normally, there are two possible fates for the newborn calves. If the calf is female she will usually be reared for dairy production like her mother; if the calf is male, he may be sold for veal production. (Veal is the word used to describe the food product derived from the flesh of calves.)

Confinement veal farming systems account for most of the veal pro-

Veal calves chained at the neck in their crates to prevent movement.

duced in the United States. In confinement veal production the calf is placed in a small crate where he is chained at the neck. The calf will spend approximately four months alone in the crate, in a darkened building, unable to turn around or to walk. He will stand or lie on slatted wood, often in his own excrement. He will be fed a liquid diet deficient in iron but replete with drugs and antibiotics twice a day. He will

One million veal calves live in crates like this and are slaughtered each year in the United States.

receive no other contact with humans or other animals except for these daily twenty minute feedings. When the fattening period is over, the calf will be forced, often by painful electric prods, to walk on weakened legs to the truck which will transport him to the slaughterhouse or stockyard.

There are several reasons for the severe conditions veal calves endure. Their movements are restricted by the chain and the crate in order to prevent them from moving around and developing muscles which would make their flesh tougher. Since veal producers want the meat to be as tender as possible, they also darken the buildings to discourage calf activity. Iron makes flesh pink. In order to keep the veal as white as possible, iron is reduced in the calves' diet. The lack of iron causes anemia in the animals. Normally, grazing on grass would provide the iron the calves require. In the crate, the calves are denied even straw bedding because they might chew on the straw and thereby obtain iron. Their liquid diet also causes them to have frequent diarrhea.

Supporters of animal protection point to this process of veal production as perhaps the most atrocious and cruel of all factory farming practices. For the sake of expensive, pale, tender veal, calves are kept anemic and denied the opportunity to walk or to interact with other calves. Those who raise calves in this manner say that the animals are protected from inclement weather and pests, that they are provided with veterinary care, and that the veal industry is fulfilling the public's demand for a delicacy. As the public learns about this kind of veal production, however, many seek out veal from humanely raised calves, or boycott the industry altogether.

Beef Cattle

Cattle raised for beef generally suffer less confinement than many other animals farmed for food, but this does not mean that their lives are pleasant. Most beef cattle are fattened in outdoor feedlots which are crowded, dirty and dusty. Feedlots are utilized because grazing land is diminishing in the United States and cannot support the huge beef industry. Feedlots serve to confine huge numbers of cattle in a relatively small area, thus facilitating the control, transportation and fattening of the animals. Many people imagine that beef cattle graze on green grass in large open fields for the duration of their lives, but increasingly more and more cows are being fattened in these barren feedlots in groups of hundreds.

As with pigs and other animals, transportation to slaughterhouses can be harsh and painful. Electric prods are used to force cows to climb into a crowded truck which will transport them to the slaughterhouse where they wait their turn for slaughter.

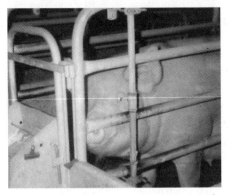

Sows in farrowing stalls are denied the opportunity to move.

Pigs

Pigs have a bad reputation in American culture. Insults comparing one to a pig, hog or sow are common. Many people perceive pigs as lazy, fat, dirty and stupid. In fact, pigs are extremely intelligent, roll in mud merely to stay cool and protected from the sun, and are bred large in order to serve as food for humans.

On some small farms, pigs are treated humanely, but in modern factory farms pigs are often confined for the duration of their lives in crowded buildings on concrete floors. The seven hundred pound animals may be placed in an area barely larger than their bodies. Sows are kept either pregnant or nursing in stalls which allow them no room to walk or move about. Such confinement is extremely debilitating to the animals. Since their feet are not designed to stand on concrete, their hooves may become deformed, causing foot, ankle and leg problems and severe pain. In addition, inhaling the toxic gases generated by the intense build-up of wastes causes many of the pigs to suffer lung damage and pneumonia.

Physical mutilations of pigs, including castration, tail docking, ear notching and teeth clipping, are common. Tail docking refers to cutting off the pigs' tails so that the pigs do not bite each others' tails. Tail biting is a neurotic behavior which occurs when pigs are in crowded, confined conditions where they are bored and

Weaned piglets are kept indoors in confinement in this factory farming facility.

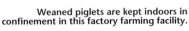

Pigs are confined in farrowing stalls when they give birth and while nursing.

frustrated. Teeth clipping is also performed to prevent damage from biting, and ear notching is practiced by some people to identify one pig from another. These procedures are rarely performed with anesthesia, and the pigs are seldom given painkillers.

Fish

Fish are either caught in nets or by hooks. With the exception of large fish the method of killing is slow suffocation on a pier or boat. Fish caught with a rod suffer the pain of the hook in their mouths before they die. Scientists have learned that fish have nerve endings in their mouths which are very sensitive, and most are convinced that the hook causes the fish pain.

Yellowfin tuna fish are caught in large nets in specific regions in the Pacific Ocean. Because commercial tuna fishers know that dolphins and tuna often swim together, they cast their nets on pods of dolphins in order to catch the tuna swimming underneath. In addition to the tuna, the nets catch and kill thousands of dolphins every year. Although federal laws have been enacted to limit the slaughter of dolphins, thousands of dolphins are still caught and killed by the United States fishing industry every year in tuna nets. In other countries even such minimal protection does not exist, and foreign companies, whose ships kill hundreds of thousands of dolphins yearly, often sell their tuna to Americans. After years of boycotts and protests, some American tuna producers have finally agreed not to purchase tuna fish who have been caught with nets.

Fish are generally caught in their natural environment, the sea or ocean, but as fish are depleted in the oceans and as pollution contaminates their bodies with dangerous toxins, a change is occurring. More and more fish are being raised on intensive, crowded fish farms.

Specialty Items

Certain gourmet foods are obtained through cruelty to animals.

Dolphin entangled in a gillnet used for fishing.

Pâté de foie gras is produced by forcing food into the gullets of geese. After the animals' livers have expanded to counteract the effects of force-feeding, the geese are killed, and their livers are removed to make the *pâté*.

The demand for frogs' legs has resulted in the capture of millions of frogs in South Asia. The frogs are often thrown into big piles and are crushed or suffocated to death. Certain species of frog are currently threatened with extinction due to the frog leg industry.

Animals Used for Clothing

Leather and pigskin are lucrative by-products of the meat industry, whereas wool is an industry unto itself. Although sheep are not killed for their fur, the conditions under which they are raised for wool are often quite harsh.

Most wool comes from Australia, where sheep are often reared on overcrowded farms. Many sheep are transported by ship alive across the oceans to other destinations. They are crowded into small crates for travel and often die of disease and stress during long journeys at sea.

Shearing can be performed carefully and humanely during the late spring months, but on large, overcrowded wool farms, proper care is often neglected. Sheep often have dirty wool around their rears. Because cleaning this wool is an expensive and time consuming activity, many sheep are forced to undergo mulesing, a process in which their fur and the top layers of the skin around their rears are shaved off. Because much of the skin is removed, the wool does not grow back. Like other mutilations, this painful procedure is performed without anesthesia or painkillers.

Not only do humans use animal skin and animal fur, we also use ani-

These sheep are being crowded onto a ship for transport across the Atlantic ocean.

mal feathers. Ducks and geese have light, soft, warm feathers called down, which humans use to stuff into jackets, pillows and comforters. Down is obtained either as a by-product of food production or from geese raised specifically for their soft feathers. In the latter case, up to one third of the goose's feathers may be pulled out of the living animal at one time. The goose is not given anesthesia or pain relief.

(For information on fur clothing see Chapter Six.)

When not outdoors, this lamb has a large stall at an animal sanctuary. Few sheep raised for wool live in such humane conditions.

Conclusion

Over five billion animals are slaughtered every year in the United States for food. While meat and milk producers offer the general public visions of cows grazing on farms and chickens pecking the ground, the reality of modern agribusiness is rarely so pretty or benign. There is no doubt that animals suffer a great deal in factory farms. Many people feel compelled to view the operations in factory farms and ascertain for themselves the humaneness of the operations. Generally, however, factory farms are hidden far from view, and most slaughterhouses will not allow visitors.

Factory farming does more than cause suffering to farm animals. Such agricultural practices have caused traditional family farmers to go out of business. In order to keep up with the mechanization and industrialization of animal agriculture, family farmers have gone into debt to purchase machinery, buildings, antibiotics and other items to compete with huge agribusiness corporations. Efforts to keep up with the agribusiness industries cause farmers such financial hardship that many of their farms fail.

A variety of vegetarian cookbooks help people prepare delicious and healthy non-animal foods.

When factory farms cause family farmers to go out of business, the large agribusiness corporations defend their practices by insisting they are merely catering to the needs of the public and are not at fault for the demise of the traditional family farm. It is ironic that many factory farms justify the intensive confine-

This cow on a traditional farm is making friends.

ment of animals on the basis of their need to meet consumer demand for animal flesh and eggs. In fact, the poultry, beef, pork, dairy and egg industries spend millions of dollars advertising their products to heighten a demand for them.

The large agribusiness corporations are also creating new breeds of farm animals through genetic manipulation. Through the insertion and deletion of genes in the animals' genetic codes, they are creating cows who produce more milk, and pigs who fatten quickly. As soon as the corporations create a new type of animal, they apply for patent protection, which means that no one else can breed such an animal without paying the corporation money in the form of royalties. This genetic engineering of animals not only threatens the integrity of the animals themselves, the patenting also threatens to put the family farmer out of business altogether (see also Chapter Nine).

Rather than participate in the cruelties which are perpetrated on animals in factory farms, many people are fighting for farm animal reform and are purchasing the flesh, eggs and milk of animals reared humanely on true family farms. It is difficult, however, for most people to distinguish between food from family and factory farms, since labels rarely indicate the source of the product.

Some people who are concerned about animals believe that killing animals for food or clothing, when non-animal alternatives exist to feed and clothe human beings, is inherently immoral. These people often boycott animal flesh altogether by becoming vegetarians. Many choose neither to eat any animal products, including eggs and dairy products, nor to wear animal products such as leather and wool. Elsewhere on the spectrum are those who limit their use of these products, but who have not given up all animal products.

By refusing to contribute monetarily to food animal production, many people believe they are decreasing the demand for, and thus the production of, food animals. These people point out that a vegetarian diet is not only readily available, but is also more ecologically sound, more efficient at feeding people, and healthier than a meat-centered diet. (For a discussion about the health and environmental hazards associated with meat-eating, see Appendix B).

Few laws exist to protect the animals used for food and clothing. If a pet owner were to treat a dog or cat the way a pig is treated in a factory farm, he or she would be accused of cruelty to animals. Legal protection may one day help animals, but such protection evolves slowly. People who feel that farming practices must be reformed can urge their senators and representatives to pass laws to protect farm animals, while at the same time boycotting foods produced in factory farms.

These dairy cows are housed on a concrete floor "dry lot."

Questions and Projects

1. Some argue that since humans are omnivores, able to eat both animal flesh and plant-based foods, there is no ethical dilemma in killing animals for food. Do you agree? If there are adequate and life-sustaining non-animal foods, do you think that it is ethical to kill animals? Explain.

2. Factory farms have developed in part to satisfy the high demand for meat and dairy products. While the meat and dairy industries certainly create demand for their products, it is the consumers' excessive reliance on animal products which perpetuates factory farming. If chickens were not raised in intense confinement, but rather were allowed the run of a barnyard, people could not expect the quantity of chicken available today. Do you think that we humans should be able to have as much chicken as we want even if it necessitates cruelty to animals? Would you be willing to modify your eating habits in light of what you have learned? Explain.

3. Trace a package of bacon from the grocery store to the farm which produced it. Research the farm and report on the conditions for animals. If you are able to do so, visit the farm for a first hand assessment.

4. Read Appendix B. Choose one statement and do some research in order to evaluate the truth of the assertion.

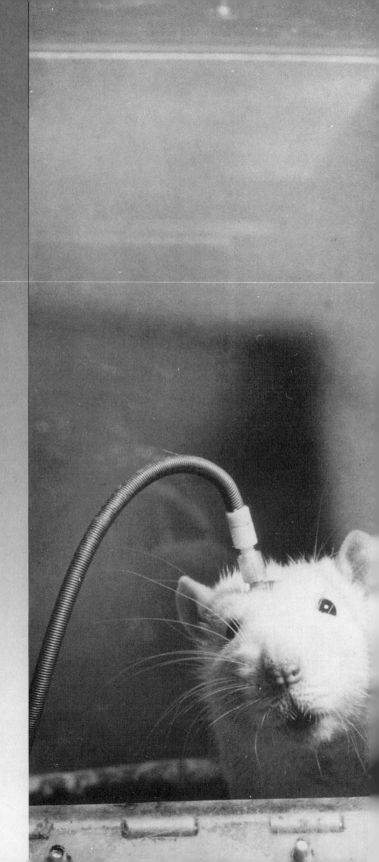

CHAPTER 9

Animals Used in Experimentation

Animal experimentation is a general term which covers a variety of activities, from testing lipstick on rabbits, to studying the effects of tobacco smoke on dogs, to trying out new drugs on mice, to practicing transplantation techniques on monkeys. Estimates place the number of animals used per year in experimentation between fifteen and seventy million.

There is much controversy regarding the usefulness of animal experimentation to human health. On one side are those who believe that current standards of human health are entirely attributable to animal experimentation. On the other side are those who believe that virtually no animal experimentation is helpful for humanity. Between these two poles lie many views. The truth is difficult to ascertain, in part because we cannot know what our society's state of health would be had more non-animal research been employed. While supporters of animal experimentation argue that the significant increase in human longevity in the twentieth century is a direct result of animal experiments, medical historians note that the great shift in longevity in the twentieth century is attributable to public health measures which caused the decline in a variety of diseases including small pox, whooping cough, diphtheria, typhoid and tuberculosis. These diseases had already declined markedly before medical interventions derived from animal experimentation were introduced to combat them.

While animal experimenters insist that animal research is necessary to cure cancer, heart disease and stroke, we now understand that these conditions are largely preventable. Despite our knowledge of preventive measures, financial and scientific resources are generally directed toward the search for cures (often relying on animal experimentation) rather than towards primary prevention of these diseases. These afflictions continue to take the lives of millions every year. In 1986, a noted Harvard scientist called "the war on cancer," initiated in 1971, a qualified failure in an article for the New England Journal of Medicine.

Since funds for health care are so limited one might well ask if our resources have been and are continuing to be directed to the appropriate areas. Perhaps if more money had been directed toward public education regarding preventive health care, the war on cancer would have been more successful.

Unfortunately, many forces work to divert money away from prevention. While many drug treatments do help people, the majority of drugs on the world market are not necessary for human health, according to the World Health Organization. Nonetheless, pharmaceutical companies continue to produce thousands of new drugs. Much of this overproduction of drugs stems from our society's focus on treating our many ailments instead of preventing them. Unnecessary production of drugs also occurs because pharmaceutical companies are part of a profit-seeking industry. Drug companies do not profit when diseases

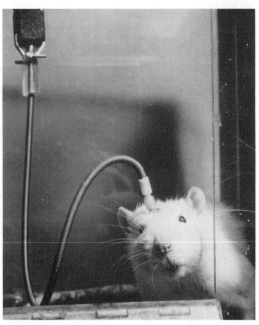

Rat in a cocaine study receives electric shocks through electrodes.

are prevented. Even many physicians and scientists have been influenced by the prevailing emphasis on cure rather than prevention.

While most people believe that animal experimentation has been of benefit to humans, the degree of benefit may be highly exaggerated by animal experimenters. In some cases, reliance on animal experimentation has actually harmed people when treatments "proven" safe on the basis of animal tests have caused irreparable damage and even fatalities in humans.

There is also experimentation which is done in the name of vanity or in the name of whiter clothes or quicker cleaning detergent, which are of questionable benefit to humans.

In addition to the question of human health benefits, there are serious ethical issues regarding animal experimentation. Is it ethical to experiment on animals against their will even if such exploitation benefits humans?

This chapter will examine the range of animal use in research and product testing, as well as the differing views regarding the morality of using animals in research and testing. These range

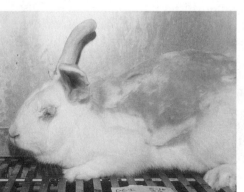

Rabbit used in eye and skin tests.

from continued use without regulatory restraints, to the three "r's" approach (reduction of numbers of animals used, refinement of techniques to ease animal suffering, and replacement of animals where possible), to the total and immediate abolition of animal experimentation.

Product Testing

The United States government requires that companies test their products for safety before placing them on the market. Government regulations do not insist upon animal tests for product safety. Many companies, however, are wary of conducting non-animal tests which the government has not specifically endorsed. Some companies claim that non-animal alternatives to provide the necessary safeguards do not exist.

It is important to note that the animal tests which are performed to ensure product safety do not necessarily keep dangerous substances off the market, nor are the results of such tests generally utilized by physicians treating patients who have become

These rabbits are being prepared for Draize eye test. They are in stocks to prevent movement and eye rubbing.

injured or ill because of a product. The tests do offer a measure of protection to the companies in the case of lawsuits brought by consumers. Companies provide test results to demonstrate that they have complied with government regulations to show the potential hazards of their products.

Virtually all products on the market must be tested for safety, including cosmetics, cleaners and other household products, glues, liquid office supplies, pesticides, soaps, lotions and even children's toys. While many companies choose cell culture, organ culture, computer and mathematical modeling, placenta analysis and other techniques in lieu of animal tests (see Appendix A), most of the large companies continue to employ animal tests in their efforts to comply with safety requirements. In recent years, however, several large cosmetic companies have stopped animal testing, and the move away from animal tests is gaining momentum.

Tests which are routinely performed on animals include the Draize rabbit eye irritancy test, the lethal dose tests, inhalation studies, and skin tests. These tests are carried out on a variety of animals such as mice, rats, guinea pigs, rabbits, hamsters, as well as on dogs and cats.

The Draize Test

In order to ascertain whether a product will irritate the human eye, a sample of the product (from shampoo to oven cleaner) is placed in one eye of a rabbit. The other eye is left alone as a control. By observing the amount of swelling, corneal damage and inflammation of the rabbit's eye, a measure of eye irritancy is established in the rabbit. The results are then applied to humans. The

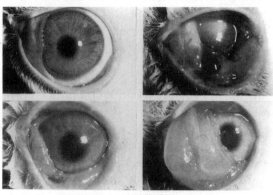

These rabbit eyes show various stages of inflammation from the Draize eye test.

rabbits used are rarely given painkillers to relieve the suffering caused by the tests.

Many ophthalmologists point out that rabbit eyes are very different from human eyes, and that the results of Draize eye tests are not necessarily applicable to humans. Some scientists have developed alternatives to the Draize test which do not require rabbits, and which are highly successful at evaluating potential irritancy. While neither animal nor non-animal tests can predict human eye irritancy perfectly, non-animal tests have proved to be quite reliable. Further developments in the field of non-animal tests will likely lead to the complete replacement of the rabbit eye irritancy test.

The Lethal Dose Tests

In order to evaluate the toxicity of substances that are taken internally, products are force-fed to animals (including rodents, rabbits, dogs, monkeys and other mammals). These tests are called lethal dose tests. "Lethal dose" refers to the amount of a given substance required to cause death. The Lethal Dose: Fifty test (LD:50) determines the amount of substance required to kill fifty percent of the animals used in a given study.

Lethal dose tests cause severe pain and suffering to animals. Even if a substance is relatively harmless, the test is designed to overdose a certain number of the animals to determine the amount which kills a specific percentage. Many animals convulse, gasp for breath and die from suffocation, heart failure, or because their insides have been chemically burned or ruptured.

Companies are ultimately responsible for the safety of their products. If a person is injured by using a product, that person may sue the company which produced it. Traditionally, animal tests have been cited to show that companies have complied with regulations to test their products for safety. Companies retain the information acquired from animal tests and place warning labels on products. These measures are taken to protect companies from losing lawsuits.

The animal tests do not necessarily protect the consumer, however. It is rare that an emergency room physician consults with lethal dose tests to treat patients who have consumed a toxic substance, nor do the safety tests keep toxic products off the market. For example, ammonia can be fatal if swallowed. Knowing the lethal dose required to kill a rat will not save a person who has swallowed ammonia.

Inhalation Tests

Certain products give off fumes either naturally or when burned which can cause lung damage, breathing difficulties, neurological damage and even cancer. In inhalation tests, animals are placed in sealed containers and are forced to breathe enormous quantities of gaseous substances until a certain percentage die. Many animals drown as their lungs fill with fluid.

As is the case with other lethal dose tests, the quantities of product forced upon animals in inhalation tests far exceed the amount which any human would ever actually encounter.

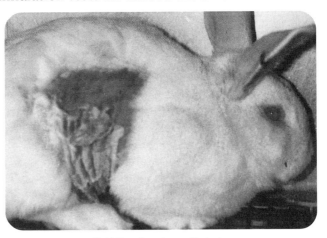

Rabbit undergoing a skin test.

Skin Tests

Many substances are evaluated in dermal irritancy tests to ascertain whether they are harmful to skin. In these tests a substance is applied to the shaved skin of an animal and held in place with tape. When the tape is removed the damage to the skin is observed. Some substances, like mild lotions, may cause little damage. Other substances, like pesticides, acidic compounds and household cleaners, may burn right through the skin causing tremendous pain and suffering to the animal. As with other tests the animals are rarely, if ever, given pain relief medication.

Summary of Product Testing

Sometimes conclusions derived from animal tests are successfully applied to humans; at other times, however, conclusions based on animal tests may be highly inaccurate when applied to humans. The non-animal tests which are now emerging may often provide more accurate results than animal tests since they utilize human cell and organ cultures and computer modeling based on human reactions (see Appendix A).

Companies may also consider the judicious use of ingredients which are already known to be safe for humans, or whose toxicity has already been ascertained, until non-animal tests are developed to indicate safety in all cases.

Recently, quite a number of companies which have relied on animal tests in the past have discontinued animal tests in favor of modern non-animal testing methods. Some of the largest cosmetic companies, such as Avon, Revlon and Estée Lauder, have joined the trend toward non-animal safety testing and have discontinued their animal tests.

Those who argue for the continued use of animal tests often claim that humans should not be "guinea pigs." They may assert that it is better to test a product on a rabbit or rat than on a human. Opponents of product testing on animals insist that there is no need to harm either humans or animals to ensure product

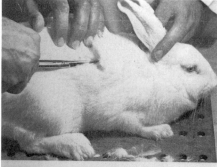
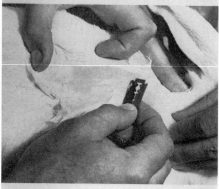
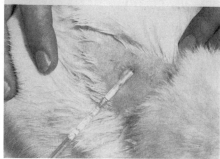

Stages of a skin test

safety. By using non-animal tests, careful clinical trials, substances known to be benign, and post-marketing surveillance, the consumer's safety can be virtually guaranteed.

Opponents of animal testing also point out that the tests are often performed in the name of new and improved products like cosmetics and household cleaners - substances which are hardly necessary for the health and well-being of the human species. They ask whether the development and promotion of such products can truly justify the cruelty and suffering that is inflicted upon animals.

Biomedical Research

Biomedical research refers both to medical research for the treatment of disease and injury, as well as to basic research to understand the biological principles of living organisms.

Over eighty-five percent of the animals used in biomedical research are mice and rats. The rest include dogs, cats, rabbits, guinea pigs, chinchillas, farm animals, monkeys, apes, birds, reptiles, amphibians and other animals. The Animal Welfare Act, a law passed by Congress in 1966 and updated as recently as 1985, provides some limited protection for laboratory animals. Under the Act research animals must be provided with appropriate cages, food, water, and proper sanitation. The regulations which have been developed to enforce the Animal Welfare Act, however, exempt mice, rats, birds and farm animals – the very animals who comprise the great majority of experimental subjects.

Further, the Act does not protect any animals from painful procedures conducted during the course of the experiments, nor does the Act require that painkillers be administered to animals if the experimenter asserts that painkillers will interfere with the design or objectives of the experiment. Because of these loopholes, many people find the Animal Welfare Act to be inadequate.

The morality of using animals in experimentation is hotly debated. Even when an experiment is carried out with humanitarian aims, the breeding, rearing, caging, and eventual killing of the animals involved raise certain ethical questions: do humans have the right to use animals to gain knowledge? to practice new surgical techniques? to test drugs meant for ourselves? to inflict animals with disease in the search for cures? to explore the

Chimpanzee used in experiments studying syphilis.

psychological problems associated with stressful situations? to try to understand the effects of human-caused disease and trauma associated with drugs, alcohol, tobacco, or the use of automobiles? to test each pharmaceutical company's version of the same new drug?

Those who support animal experimentation claim that it is immoral *not* to conduct animal studies if there is any possibility that humans will benefit from them. They insist that our increased longevity, improved health, and virtually all the major medical advances of the twentieth century are attributable to animal experimentation. They ask us to imagine how many millions of people would have died from diabetes, polio, leukemia and other afflictions had there been no experiments with animals.

This line of reasoning revolves around several assumptions: that the interests of humans are more important than the interests of non-human animals, that animals may be exploited to serve human ends, and that other methods and strategies for medical advancement did and do not exist. Many advocates of animal experimentation would prefer that *no* further restrictions be placed on animal experimentation, and quite a few have opposed and obstructed even minimal improvements sought by the United States Congress.

Some doctors, scientists and others traditionally supportive of animal experimentation, however, do agree with animal advocates that more careful scrutiny of research grants is necessary in order to avoid trivial or duplicative experiments. Some also feel that strict laws

Chained and caged monkeys to be used in experiments.

should protect the well-being, both physical and psychological, of experimental subjects. In fact, several organizations have been formed by health professionals concerned about promoting responsible research and animal welfare in the laboratory setting (see Appendix D).

Many animal advocates agree that some benefits have been and may be derived from animal experimentation, but they insist that the gains attributed to animal experiments are highly exaggerated. Some also argue that human health would be *better* overall if more alternative, non-animal studies and health initiatives had been conducted. These people ask us to imagine how many millions of people would be alive today had medical science concentrated on the *prevention* of the three major disease killers of our time, heart disease, cancer and stroke, instead of focusing on the search for cures based on animal experiments. They point out that for 98% of all forms of cancer there has been no significant increase in survival during the past twenty years. Had the billions of dollars spent on animal research during those twenty years been spent on public education regarding preventive health care, up to 70% of those cancer victims might never have become ill.

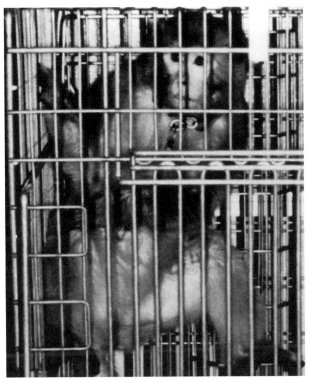

This young monkey will be used in an experiment.

Those critical of animal experiments also believe that surgical techniques and curative drugs could still have been developed without animal experimentation. Perhaps individuals suffering from a fatal disease, or requiring a particular surgical procedure in order to survive, would have been the "guinea pigs" for new drug therapies or surgical techniques. This kind of work does go on today through a process known as informed consent, whereby patients agree to try a new treatment and are made aware that there may be some risks involved.

Unfortunately, American law often prevents sick people from trying new treatments which have not been tested on animals. Many AIDS patients, for example, have been denied the right to try new drugs which have not been tested on animals. These people have been fight-

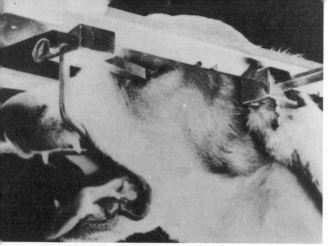

Stereotaxic devices such as this immobilize animals so that they will not move during experimental procedures.

ing for the right to try new treatments as they are developed. Such human trials would not only offer them a chance to live, they would also provide the most accurate information for the treatment of others.

Animal advocates insist that it is immoral to create a slave population from other species. They feel that even if the claims that animal experimentation is highly beneficial are accurate, the exploitation of other species is still unethical. Unlike animal experimenters, animal rights advocates do not draw a distinct line between human and nonhuman animals when it comes to moral consideration. While each person draws a line somewhere (few would take the interests of single-celled creatures seriously for instance), animal advocates believe that the basis for considering the rights or interests of an animal lies with the animal's ability to suffer and feel pain or, conversely, to experience satisfaction or pleasure.

Scientists have discovered that human and nonhuman animals are similar in their capacity to suffer physical and psychological pain. That is one reason why animals are used in pain experiments and psychological studies. Animals exhibit many of the same responses as humans who are in pain or who are frightened, and they struggle to stay alive with as much intensity as humans. Common sense tells us that animals clearly feel pain and fear much the way humans do. Because of these similarities between human and nonhuman animals, animal advocates do not arbitrarily place nonhuman animals outside the realm of moral consideration.

Animal advocates also point out that many animals, such as primates and dogs, are more conscious, intelligent and aware than some severely retarded, senile, or otherwise afflicted humans. Rejecting experimental procedures on humans with such disabilities, they also reject such procedures on animals. They argue that placing human interests above any consideration of animal interests is speciesist and akin to placing white people's interests above blacks (racist), men's interests above women's (sexist), or wealthy people's interests above poor people's (classist).

Many of these people would like to see animal experiments phased out completely.

There are others who feel that strict guidelines should be established to prevent the unnecessary repetition of animal studies, trivial experiments on animals, and/or painful experiments on animals. These people would like all animals used in laboratories to be provided with psychological and physical comforts and appropriate veterinary attention to prevent any pain or stress.

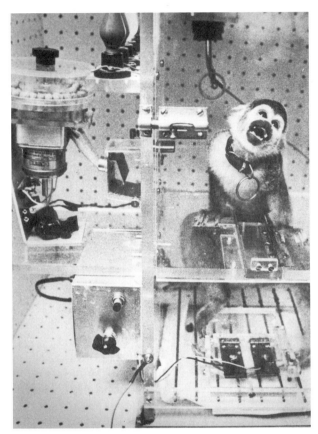

This monkey is being utilized in a study of alcoholism conducted by the United States Army.

Military Experiments

The military has a long history of animal experimentation. Animals are subjected to nuclear radiation, poison, burns, rifle wounds, blood loss, temperature extremes and psychological stress tests. Monkeys and cats have been force-fed LSD and other hallucinogens; explosives have been detonated on fully conscious goats; cats have been shot in the head; dogs' legs have been broken, and unanesthetized pigs have been burned to the muscle with blow torches. These tests have been conducted by the Department of Defense in its desire to better prepare soldiers for battle, to treat humans who have been injured in war, to develop more lethal weapons, and to explore the effects of chemical, biological and nuclear agents on living organisms.

Examples of Other Experiments

It would be impossible to document all of the experiments on animals which are conducted by the biomedical research community. Billions of tax dollars are spent yearly on animal experiments. A brief sampling must suffice:

•Animals are killed and their cells are examined to better understand biochemistry and physiology.

•Dogs and monkeys are forced to endure shocks and other painful stimuli to better understand psychological responses to unalleviated

pain and stress.
  •Animals are forced to inhale cigarette smoke to show the effects of smoking.
  •Animals are forced to become drug or alcohol addicts in the search for treatments for drug addiction and alcoholism.
  •Animals are injected with viruses and disease agents in order to test drug treatments.
  •Animals are deprived of food, water, or maternal companionship in an effort to understand

Cirrhosis of liver induced by drugs.

deprivation of these necessities in humans.
  •Animals are burned to better understand how to treat burns.
  •Human genes are introduced into animals, and other genetic manipulations are performed on them to develop laboratory animals more susceptible to certain diseases and farm animals who produce more meat or milk.

Conclusion

The issue of animal experimentation is very complex. Only those who believe that all animal experimentation is morally wrong or scientifically invalid, and those who believe that all research is justified no matter what pain and suffering is caused and for whatever dubious gain, have easy answers. The rest of the population is often confused by assertions from both the animal experimenters and the animal rights advocates.

You are encouraged to develop your own opinion and to scrutinize all of the perspectives detailed above.

Questions and Projects

  1. Obtain copies of current bills concerning animal experimentation before your state and national Congresses (see Appendix G)

and write or call your senators and representatives to inquire about the pending legislation. Research the bills and inform your legislators of your opinion.

2. Organize a debate on the subject of animal experimentation and testing. Choose sides and research your side thoroughly. After the debate, switch sides and repeat. Write down your personal conclusions based on your experience.

3. There are some animal rights activists who break into laboratories and steal animals, videotapes, documents and computer disks. In some cases the stolen film footage and documentation have provided evidence of cruelty to animals and infractions of the Animal Welfare Act. What is your opinion about breaking the law to rescue experimental animals or to document cruelty and wrong-doing to animals? Upon what criteria do you base your conclusion?

4. Consider a circumstance, or research an historical event, in which you would support illegal activity on behalf of humans. How does this exercise affect your opinion about illegal activities on behalf of animals?

5. Do you think that animal experimentation is inherently immoral or not? Explain.

6. Obtain a copy of the Animal Welfare Act (and the regulations for its enforcement) as well as the National Institutes of Health Guide for the Care and Use of Laboratory Animals. These documents may be requested free of charge from your federal senators or representative. After reading the documents, consider the following questions: How adequate do you think the regulations are in protecting animals? Do you think that these regulations meet the animals' needs? Would you keep your own animals under the conditions required by the regulations?

CHAPTER 10

Animals Considered to be Pests

There are certain animals that many people do not like. While some of these animals may be parasites, threatening people or domestic animals, others may actually be helpful to humans. For example, snakes, bats and spiders are particularly useful animals to have on a farm because they eat other animals who threaten crops. Nonetheless, many people fear and dislike these usually benign creatures.

This chapter examines the concept of "pests" and considers the differences between parasites, that actually threaten human survival, and harmless creatures who are disliked simply because of their physical appearance or habits.

Rodents

Mice and rats are perhaps the two most maligned mammals in our society. In some cases the fear of rats is warranted. Many people who live in cities with dense populations of rats have suffered rat bites. Rats have also been known to spread diseases.

Often, city governments as well as individual citizens respond to rat infestations by putting out rat poison. Rat poisons are not only dangerous substances, they also cause tremendous animal suffering. Rats who ingest poison-laced food endure slow and painful deaths. The dead rats may then become food for other animals, including dogs, cats, raccoons and opossums who also die because of the poison residues left in the rats. Even children can become the victims of rat poison if they play near poisoned areas.

Rat poisons are only moderately effective. Many rats die quickly, but more rats come to take their place. A more effective way to rid an area of rats is to make the area less appealing to them. People who think that rat poisons are cruel and environmentally hazardous suggest that more money be directed toward improved housing and sanitation in areas with rat infestations so that homes and neighborhoods will not attract rats.

Mice are much less threatening than rats to human health, but they may still be nuisances. People do not like to share their homes with mice who crawl into cupboards, get into food, and leave droppings around the kitchen. Few consider the well-being of the mouse when they lay out a trap.

Mousetraps are generally of two varieties: the spring version kills swiftly by breaking the mouse's neck, while the glue trap works slowly as the mouse struggles, unable to get away, but still fully conscious. Eventually, the mice die of dehydration or starvation on glue traps, or are killed by those individuals who have put out the traps.

Alternative humane traps are now available which are designed to catch the mice in a small mouse house for removal outdoors (see Appendix A). These traps may be more expensive than the traps which kill, but because they can be used over and over again, their cost is ultimately less than that of kill traps.

Prairie dogs are being exterminated by farmers and ranchers. Due to the loss of prairie dogs, the black-footed ferrets who hunt the prairie dogs are becoming extinct.

Large Mammals

Raccoons, opossums, coyotes, skunks, foxes, deer and other large mammals are often considered nuisances. In some cases these animals do pose a threat to human health. Raccoons, foxes, bats and skunks are the predominant carriers of rabies in the United States, and in areas where rabies threatens human and animal health, wariness regarding these animals is neither surprising nor unjustified.

Some people think that raccoons are pests.

Some people, however, dislike these animals because they may occasionally attack chickens or other farm animals, or because they feed on crops or on decorative shrubbery and flowers, or because they overturn outdoor garbage cans, or because they smell.

For all animals on the earth, including raccoons, deer, and coyotes, habitat is decreasing rapidly. Fields and forests are being destroyed to make room for shopping malls and housing developments. Where once there was a gnarled old maple tree, there is now a house. A raccoon mother may build her nest in the attic of that house because her nest in the maple tree has been destroyed. Perhaps an exterminator is called to kill the raccoon and rid the attic of the unwanted guest.

We often fail to realize that humans have encroached upon the animals' land, not the other way around. Many people who recognize this fact take great pains to treat unwanted visitors with respect. Rather than shoot, poison or otherwise injure unwanted animals, these people will reinforce their homes, screen their chimneys, seal their garbage cans, put fences around their gardens and even plant special shrubs, bushes and crops for the animals who have been displaced. If animals do become great nuisances, some people will lay traps which catch the animals alive, for transport to a location where they will not bother humans.*

Stray Cats and Dogs

Many unwanted dogs and cats become strays. Strays may reproduce on the streets, spread diseases such as rabies, form threatening packs, bark or cry in the night, and become aggressive in their search for food. When these problems occur people may put out poison-laced food or shoot the animals. Some people may even become incensed that the government is not ridding the streets of these pests. The solution to stray cats and dogs is simple, however. People should prevent pets from breeding and should never abandon a pet (see Chapter Three).

Insects

In a concerted effort to rid the world of undesirable insects, corporations have produced pesticides. Pesticides are poisonous chemicals designed to kill certain kinds of insects. Because pesticides are poisons they may also affect animals other than insects, or insects that are not harmful. Humans are also endangered because pes-

Stray animals may get into garbage cans, become aggressive and carry diseases.

*It is important to remember that one should not trap animals once a nest with young has been established. If the mother is trapped, the newborns will die without her.

ticides often contaminate food and water supplies. When pesticides are sprayed on a field of corn, residues remain in the corn. When the corn is fed to cows, the residues remain in the flesh and milk of the cows. When people eat cow flesh or drink cow milk, these pesticide residues are ingested too.

Not only can pesticides be dangerous to humans and many other animals, they also do not work very well. The small percentage of insects resistant to a certain pesticide reproduce more insects with resistances to the poisonous chemicals. The pesticide manufacturers then produce even more potent poisons. The result of this escalation of pesticide production is more toxic residues in our foods (with the most toxic levels to be found in meat and dairy products and the least toxic levels in grains and vegetables) as well as harmful residues which have leached into our air and water supplies. (See also Appendix B.)

Our dislike of certain animal pests has resulted in behavior dangerous to our own species. By attempting to eliminate all insects which cause minor destruction, we have created a world in which major biocide through chemical poisons threatens both humans and nonhumans alike.

One encouraging development is that more and more farmers and gardeners are abandoning pesticides in favor of organic gardening where no chemical fertilizers, herbicides or pesticides are used. Many consumers are also seeking out organic produce from local farmers and grocers.

Despite the growing concern about them, pesticides are still being used, and their residues are still in our air and water supplies. The United States has banned certain pesticides because of their dangerous effects on the environment. For example, the pesticide DDT was responsible for the deaths of much wildlife, including endangered eagles.

When a pesticide is banned in the United States, however, the manufacturers may still sell the pesticide in other countries where there are no prohibitions on its sale. The pesticide will continue to hurt people, kill animals and threaten the global environment in those other countries. Ironically, the United States will also purchase food products from these same countries which are utilizing pesticides banned in America.

Conclusion

Our dislike of certain animals has resulted in activities which have dire consequences. Not only have humans been guilty of cruelty toward animals, we have also been guilty of threatening the purity of the air, water, food, and natural habitats upon which all creatures, human and nonhuman, rely. Humans can and must recognize the connections between all life, and realize that if people destroy the habitats of millions of animals, and pollute the earth in an effort to destroy those animals we dislike, our rash acts will carry consequences.

Before we consider an animal a pest and act to rid ourselves of the "nuisance," we must ask ourselves whether that characterization is fair and just, or irrational, selfish and, ultimately, mutually destructive.

This water snake is harmless to people.

Questions and Projects

1. Write down a list of animals whom you do not like. In each case, consider whether your dislike is rational (the animal may threaten you) or irrational (you dislike the animal because of shape, color, behavior, etc.).
2. Research your local grocery stores to ascertain the percentage of organically grown fruits and vegetables. Can you find any organic animal products (products from animals who were fed organically produced foods)?
3. Humans are destroying more and more animal habitat annually in order to build houses, shopping centers, and other buildings. What solutions can you suggest to help diminish the destruction of animal habitat?
4. Choose an animal whom humans think of as a pest and write a story about the animal's life from the animal's point of view.

CHAPTER 11

The Future for Planet Earth

We are at a pivotal moment in history. The late twentieth century is witnessing a turning point. Will humanity reverse the destructive habits which threaten life on earth, or will we continue our short-sighted behaviors and leave behind a wasteland? The decisions which the next generation of humans make may be the decisions which determine the fate of our planet and all the creatures who inhabit it.

Human overpopulation, rainforest destruction, air and water pollution, depletion of natural resources, habitat destruction, global warming and nuclear power and weapon production all threaten life on earth. This chapter examines the planetary destruction which is occurring on a massive scale and calls for a new ethic which will save our planet and the creatures who live on it.

Extinction

Throughout our planet's history, extinction has been a natural process. Many plants and animals which once inhabited the earth are recorded now only as fossils. The dinosaurs roamed the planet for millions of years, then disappeared. The many extinctions which occur now, however, are rarely part of a natural process. Human interference with the well-being of the planet has caused the rate and extent of extinction to increase dramatically.

Many of our earth's large mammals are endangered. Whales, elephants, rhinoceroses, apes, and many other animals are losing their natural habitats. Thousands of animal species are disappearing as the rainforests are razed and destroyed all over the earth. Most of the rainforest species are insects. These animals do not capture the attention of the public or of legislators, but they are vital to our planet's good health.

Unless we stop destroying the environment, we will continue to cause the extinction of thousands of animals. If we do not stop our destructive behaviors, animals may only be preserved in zoos.

The Rainforests

Rainforests exist in a complex equilibrium. Unlike temperate zone forests, if the trees are razed in a rainforest, they do not grow back. Like animals, rainforests can become extinct.

There are several reasons why rainforests are being destroyed. In some places, people have responded to the economic incentive to raise cattle for beef to sell to foreign industries and fast food restaurants. Rainforests in these regions are being destroyed to graze cattle. As the human population

A logger cuts down a tree in the rainforest.

swells and more people try to find ways to feed themselves, some seek out the razed forests for vegetable and grain agriculture. The soil in a rainforest is not suitable for either animal or vegetable agriculture, however. Without the rich nutrients channeled through

This rainforest in Costa Rica is protected from logging by funds from concerned people all over the world.

the trees and plants, the sandy soil is unable to produce grass or crops for long. After only a few years, what was once a rich and living system is dead. The short-term benefit to a few humans is obtained at the expense of the rainforests, the earth, and all of the forests' inhabitants.

Another tragedy associated with rainforest destruction is the hardship suffered by those farmers who have moved to the rainforests to raise cattle or grow crops. When the crops stop growing, these farmers and their families suffer greatly.

Global Warming

Trees and plants breathe. The green plants of the earth breathe in carbon dioxide and breathe out oxygen. Humans and other animals need oxygen to survive. As the rainforests are destroyed the levels of oxygen in the atmosphere may decrease. Not only will there be less oxygen to breathe, there will also be too much carbon dioxide.

Increased carbon dioxide and other gases in the atmosphere affect the earth's ability to maintain its temperature. Buildup of these gases causes the atmosphere to behave like a greenhouse, trapping warm air close to the

Tree stumps are all that remain of a rainforest burned so the land could be used by farmers.

surface of the planet. This process is called global warming.

Slight increases in temperature cause drastic changes in weather patterns. Environmental scientists are predicting that global warming will cause the melting of icecaps (resulting in floods which will destroy coastal cities), heavy droughts, extinction of much plant and animal life, and many other irreparable changes.

Waste management incinerators produce toxic gases and ash.

Rainforest destruction is not the only cause of increased carbon dioxide in the atmosphere. The burning of fossil fuels, such as gasoline, emits huge quantities of carbon dioxide and dangerous gases into the air. The United States is guilty of burning more fossil fuels, through industry, automobiles, animal agriculture and other activities, than any other country in the world.

In order to slow the process of global warming, we must decrease our reliance on fossil fuels as well as find alternative clean energy sources.

Acid Rain

The automotive and other industries are responsible for more than just global warming. Every time a car engine begins to run, gases are emitted through its exhaust system into the atmosphere. These gases combine with water molecules in clouds and return to the earth in the form of highly acidic rain. Acid rain, as it is called, destroys trees, ruins lakes and ponds, and kills animal and plant life.

The vicious cycle of planetary destruction continues as the trees succumb to acid rain

Trees destroyed by acid rain.

and die, thereby contributing further to global warming and animal habitat loss.

Pollution

Car emissions and factories not only cause acid rain, they also pollute the air, making breathing difficult. Large cities are notorious for their hovering clouds of smog and their frequent media warnings concerning poor air quality.

Garbage strewn all over a beach in Atlantic City, NJ.

Pollution occurs on many levels. Poisonous chemicals are introduced into the environment as by-products of many industries, from paper mills to paint producing companies. Sometimes companies are guilty of intentionally dumping toxins into the water or on land, but even when companies comply with anti-pollution laws, toxins may still get into our food, water and air. For example, the process of bleaching paper often produces dioxins, which are particularly poisonous chemicals. When the bleached paper is then used to make milk cartons, the dioxins sometimes leach out of the paper and into the milk.

This sea bird is covered with oil from an oil spill.

Pollution cannot be contained within political borders. DDT has been found in the breast milk of Inuit (Eskimo) women; fish deep in the ocean have been found to contain dangerous levels of mercury; medical wastes dumped into the ocean near New York City drift onto shore in New Jersey, and the accident at the nuclear power plant in Chernobyl in the Soviet Union is still affecting the health of both people and farm animals in Scandanavia and Eastern Europe.

It is not only corporations and industries which pollute the earth. We live in a society of disposable products and massive proliferation of unnecessary items. Whether we eat at fast food restaurants and throw out the paper, plastic and styrofoam packaging, or use disposable instead of cloth diapers, or carry our groceries home in plastic or paper bags instead of reusable canvas sacks, we ourselves are contributing to the pollution of our planet.

Part of Lake Ontario too polluted to swim in.

Our wasteful habits are catching up with us. We are running out of room to bury our wastes, so some countries are burning them, emitting dangerous pollutants and producing poisonous ash. Whether through oil spills, nuclear bomb tests, styrofoam and plastic wastes, or chemical dumping, humans are treating the earth like a garbage can.

Natural Resource Depletion

Humans are depleting the earth's natural resources at an alarming rate. Ores and fossil fuels are disappearing quickly causing periodic economic upheavals and intermittent shortages. The vicious cycle of planetary destruction shows itself in this arena as in others. As resources become scarce, more effort is made to find additional sources of these precious items. Ocean drilling, strip mining and other methods for finding and obtaining natural resources cause great damage to the earth and its inhabitants.

Nuclear Energy

Our world is in the midst of an energy crisis. As we deplete the earth of natural resources, we are facing the problem of not having enough energy to run our cars, factories and refrigerators, or to heat our homes and our water, or to light our buildings. Because we are facing the loss of fossil fuels in the coming century, many people are searching for other energy sources, such as solar (sun) power, wind power and water power.

Our society has not spent much money on developing these safe and renewable energies, however. Instead, we have built nuclear power plants and continued the search and drilling for oil in fragile ecosystems. Most people have heard about some of the dangers associated with nuclear power because there have been many nuclear power plant accidents throughout the world in which dangerous radioactive substances have been released into the air and water.

It is not only the threat of accidents which makes nuclear power unsafe. Nuclear power plants also produce toxic waste. We do not have any safe place to put the waste, and currently, much of it is buried in the earth in barrels. These radioactive wastes take thousands of years to become harmless, but the barrels which contain the wastes may last less than one hundred years. If the wastes leach out of the barrels and get into our water supplies, we will face dangerous radioactive pollution which could destroy much of life on earth.

Animal Agriculture

Animal agriculture is responsible for natural resource depletion, air and water pollution, and much human disease. Animal agriculture contributes to massive topsoil depletion which results in "dead land." It is also extremely inefficient. It takes five to fifteen pounds of grain protein fed to animals to produce one pound of animal protein fed to humans. Instead of feeding corn, oats, soybeans and other grains to animals, we could be feeding them to people. Were animal agriculture discontinued, land would be available to produce enough vegetables and grains to feed the entire population of humans who are starving on the planet, and the crops could be more effectively rotated to slow topsoil depletion.

There are no sewage systems to treat and dispose of animal wastes, so millions of tons of animal waste currently pollute land, water and even air. Although it is not widely publicized, animal wastes are a major source of environmental pollution in the United States.

A tremendous amount of fossil fuels are required to run the machinery necessary for animal agriculture, to heat the buildings which house the animals, to transport the animals and to refrigerate the animal meat. The burning of these fuels uses up a natural resource and pollutes the earth. (For detailed statistics on health and environmental hazards associated with animal agriculture see Appendix B.)

Human Overpopulation

Humans are reproducing at a rate the earth cannot sustain. We have populated every corner of the planet, even venturing into the most inhospitable of regions. All of the destruction humans are wreaking on the planet can be attributed to overpopulation. Animal habitats disappear because humans require more land; the rainforests are razed because humans seek more space, more wood, and more food. Global warming progresses because more and more humans burn more and more fuel and cut down more and more trees. Billions of animals are raised and slaughtered to sate the appetites of an expanding population. The protective ozone layer of our atmosphere is depleted as more humans spray more aerosol and produce more ozone-destroying chemicals in the styrofoam, air-conditioning and refrigeration industries. More humans drive more cars contributing to more acid rain. More humans require more products contributing to more air and water pollution. More humans produce more wastes.

Recycling cans like this one help people to recycle their bottles, cans, newspapers and other materials.

The problem lies in the word "more;" the solution lies with the word "less." Only when we humans commit ourselves to less consumption, and only when population growth is at zero can humanity hope to solve our planetary problems. At the rate we are consuming and reproducing, little can be done to reverse the destruction of the earth.

What Can We Do?

In order to slow the pace of planetary destruction, we must alter our behaviors and develop and live by a new ethic – an ethic of interdependence, responsibility, compassion, and long-term planning.

• We can improve the energy efficiency of our vehicles, revamp our public transportation systems, create workspaces which are close to our homes and continue the search for clean fuel which is replenishable.

• We can walk, ride our bikes, carpool, or take public transportation whenever possible.

• We can reduce our overall consumption, recycle our wastes, and reconsider the belief system which encourages people to fulfill every whim for material goods. We can build fewer shopping centers and malls and leave the land for animals and plants.

• We can take care not to waste water by turning off faucets, watering lawns at night or early in the morning, taking shorter showers, and eating lower on the food chain.

• We can use cloth diapers instead of disposable diapers.

• We can avoid disposable products in general.

• We can grow vegetables in our own gardens and insist on organic foods at our markets. We can shop with reusable cloth bags instead of using disposable plastic or paper bags. We can buy only what we need with as little packaging as possible. We can also buy products produced nearby rather than those transported across long distances.

• We can eat lower on the food chain by becoming vegetarians and thereby alleviate extreme animal suffering, much human illness, and tremendous environmental degradation.

• We can elect legislators who are committed to ensuring the survival of the planet and the millions of species who reside on earth.

• We can resolve to consider how our behavior affects not just ourselves, our families and our friends, but also how our behavior affects the planet and the other animals who share the earth with us.

• We can commit ourselves to a zero population growth strategy, understanding that the earth cannot sustain any more people.

Questions and Projects

1. Choose a company (paper producer, automotive company, fast food restaurant, upholstery producer, building developer, chemical manufacturer etc.) and research how that company's activity is contributing to environmental destruction and animal suffering. Write up a list of pros and cons for the company: for example, how does the production of the company's product(s) contribute to society versus how does the production cause harm to people, animals and/or the environment.

2. Examine your own habits and choose one behavior that is harmful to the environment and/or to animals which you are willing to change. (Remember to pick a behavior which you will truly be able to alter!) Make a commitment to change your behavior. When you are ready, choose another habit to change.

3. Design a small city or town which is self-sustaining and which is environmentally sound. Identify the industries present in the town, the distances between homes and workplaces, etc.

4. Keep a notebook in which you record the many ways in which the earth is being degraded and destroyed. Take time to observe and note environmental problems in your own region.

Remember, we cannot change our behaviors until we become aware of the problems.

5. When the Exxon Valdez spilled oil in the clean waters off the coast of Alaska, the public was enraged. Who is responsible for this disaster: the captain of the ship, the Chief Executive Officer of Exxon, or the public which has demanded such great quantities of oil? Discuss.

APPENDIX A
Non-Animal Alternatives and Methods in Research and Testing

PARTIAL LIST OF NON-ANIMAL RESEARCH METHODS

The Ames Test: The Ames Test utilizes bacteria to detect mutagens (chemicals that induce genetic mutations). Because mutations are often associated with the development of cancer, the Ames test is used as a screen for carcinogenicity. This test takes only a few days to perform and costs a few hundred dollars.

Audiovisual Guides and Aids: These offer the advantage of repeated viewing and allow the viewer to study procedures on human patients instead of animals.

Bacteria Cultures and Protozoan Studies: Protozoa have a similar chemistry to that of humans and are useful in many areas of research.

The Chorioallantoic Membrane (CAM) Test: The CAM test utilizes membranes from chicken eggs to evaluate toxicity and is a prominent alternative to the Draize test. This procedure causes no pain.

Computer-Assisted Drug Design: This drug development strategy utilizes three-dimensional graphics and quantum pharmacology based on the "lock-and-key" mechanism of drug action.

Computer Simulations: Both time and cost-efficient in their ability to screen out potentially harmful substances in early testing stages, computer simulations provide considerable information not obtainable from experiments using live animals.

Gas Chromatography and Mass Spectrometry: These techniques are used in identifying drugs and chemical substances through the study of chemical and drug activity at the molecular level.

Genetic Engineering: This new technology is now being used to produce an improved, purer type of insulin. Growth hormone and interferon can also be produced through the same method.

Human Studies: *Clinical* – These involve the study of sick or injured patients, incorporating healthy volunteers as controls. *Epidemiological* – Epidemiological studies analyze information on large numbers of people to uncover potential relationships between the incidence of disease or injury and people's habits or environments. *Post mortem* – These involve the study of cadavers donated to science. *Post mortem* studies are particularly useful in anatomical and transplant research. Cadavers are also sources of transplantable organs.

Imaging Techniques: These methods generate visual images of the body's interior, without the need for invasive procedures, and are now being used to study the human brain in action. One such technique, positron emission tomography (PET), utilizes tiny amounts of radioactive chemicals to mark areas of interest in the brain. PET has recently been applied in the study of Parkinson's Disease.

Mathematical Models: These models combine existing information to describe a system under study in mathematical terms. This approach results in a mathematical model helpful in the understanding of complicated systems, especially those in which several variables influence an outcome.

Organ Cultures: This is an emerging new field which uses groups of cells from a single organ for cancer research, pharmacology, radiation, toxicology, virus research, vaccine production and other areas of research.

Physical and Chemical Techniques: Using physiochemical instruments that isolate, identify and measure the amount of a given substance in complex biological mixtures, these techniques analyze the physical and chemical properties of drugs, toxins, body chemicals, and other substances.

Placenta: The placenta, which is usually discarded after childbirth, is a complex, multipurpose organ that is highly sensitive to drugs, chemicals and pollutants. The placenta may also be utilized for practicing microsurgery.

Quantum Pharmacology: Quantum pharmacology is a discipline which utilizes quantum mechanics to explain the behavior of drugs on the basis of their molecular composition.

Tissue Cultures: Tissue culture techniques are utilized in biomedical research, particularly in studies of the immune system. Individual cells from human or animal tissues are grown outside the body after separation from their original tissue or organ. Each generation breeds identical cells almost without limit, thus providing a continuous supply of identical test materials.

COMPANIES WHICH DO NOT TEST PRODUCTS ON ANIMALS

Abracadabra, Inc., P.O. Box 1040, Guerneville, CA 95446

Advance Design Laboratories, P.O. Box 55016, Metro Station, Los Angeles, CA 90055

Alfin Fragrances, Inc., 15 Maple St., Norwood, NJ 07648

Alva–Amco Pharmacal Cosmetics, 6625 Avondale Ave., Chicago, IL 60631

Amberwood, Rt. 1, P.O. Box 206, Milner, GA 30257

American Cosmetic Mfg. Labs, Inc., 500 4th St., San Francisco, CA 91340

Andalina, Tory Hill, Warner, NH 03278–0057

Aroma Vera, P.O. Box 3609, Culver City, CA 90231

Aubrey Organics, 4419 N. Manhattan Ave., Tampa, FL 33614

Aura Cacia, Inc., P.O. Box 3157, Santa Rosa, CA 95402

Auromere, Ayurvedic Imports, 1291 Weber St., Pomona, CA 91768

Autumn–Harp, Inc., 28 Rockydale Rd., Bristol, VT 05443

Aveda, 321 Lincoln St. NE, Minneapolis, MN 55413

Avon Products, Inc., 9 W. 57th St., New York, NY 10019

Baby Touch, Ltd., 135 El Condor Ct., San Rafael, CA 94903

Beauty Without Cruelty, 190 Pool St., Biddeford, MA 04005

Belvedere Labs, 20688 Corsair Blvd., Hayward, CA 94544

Biddeford Industries, Inc., P.O. Box 408, Biddeford, MA 04005

Bio Line, Inc., 9201 Penn. Ave. S. Suite 26, Minneapolis, MN 55431

Biokosma, 841 S. Main St., Spring Valley, NY 10977

CW Bodkins, Ltd., 228 2nd Ave. SW, Pacifica, WA 98047

Body Love, P.O. Box 2711, Petaluma, CA 94953

The Body Shop, 45 Horsehill Rd., Hanover Technical Center Cedar Knolls, NJ 07927–2003

Borlind of Germany, P.O. Box 307, Grantham, NJ 03753

C&S Laboratories, 5600 G McLeod Ave., Albuquerque, NM 87109

Carbona Products Co., 330 Calyer St., Brooklyn, NY 11222

Caring Cosmetics, P.O. Box 103, Harvey Cedars, NJ 08008

Celestial Seasonings, Inc., 1780 55th St., Boulder, CO 80301

Chenti Products, Inc., 21093 Forbes Ave., Hayward, CA 94545

Clientele, 5207 NW 163rd St., Miami, FL 33014

Columbia Manicure Mfg. Co., 1 Seneca Place, Greenwich, CT 06830

Comfort Mfg. Co., 1056 W. Van Buren St., Chicago, IL 60607

Community Soap Factory, P.O. Box 32057, Washington, DC 20007

Compassion Cosmetics, Debbie Ryan, P.O. Box 3534, Glendale, CA 91201

Compassion Products, 718 Crane St., Catasaqua, PA 18032

Country Comfort, 215 Classic Ct., Rohnert Park, CA 94928

Creature Care, 9009 South St., Monte Rio, CA 95462

Cumberland Mfg. Co., P.O. Box 23830, Nashville, TN 37202

Desert Essence, 1732 Arteique Rd., Topanga, CA 90290

Diversey Wyandotte Corp., 1532 Biddle Ave., Wyandotte, MI 48192

Dodge Chemical Co. Inc., 165 Rindge Ave. Ext., Cambridge, MA 02140

Dr. EH Bronner, P.O. Box 28, Escondido, CA 92025

Dr. Hauschka Cosmetics, Inc., Meadowbrook West, Wyoming, RI 02898

Earthrite, 23700 Mercantile Rd., Beachwood, Ohio 44122–5955

Earth Science, Inc., P.O. Box 1925, Corona, CA 91720

Estée Lauder, Inc., 350 S. Service Rd., Melville, NY 11746
Fabergé, Inc., 1345 Ave. of the Americas, New York, NY 10105
Fashion Two Twenty, Inc., 1263 S. Chillicothe Rd., Aurora, OH 44202
Faultless Starch/Bon Ami Co., 1025 W. 8th St., Kansas City, MO 64100
Fleur De Sante, Inc., P.O. Box 16090, Ft. Lauderdale, FL 33318
AJ Funk & Co., 1471 Timber Dr., Elgin, IL 60120
General Nutrition, 1301 39th St., Fargo, ND 58107
Golden Lotus, Inc., P.O. Box 19366, Denver, CO 80219
Golden Star, Inc., P.O. Box 12539, N. Kansas City, MO 64116
Granny's Old Fashioned Products, 3581 E. Milton St., Pasadena, CA 91107
Gruene Kosmetik, 256 South Robertson Blvd., Beverly Hills, CA 90211
Hain Pure Food Co., 13660 S. Figuera, Los Angeles, CA 90061
Hawaiian Resources, 1123 Kapahulu Ave., Honolulu, HI 96816
Heavenly Soap, 5948 E. 30th St., Tucson, AZ 85711
Home Service Products Co., 230 Willow St., Bound Brook, NJ 08805
Humphreys Pharmaceutical, Inc., 63 Meadow Rd., Rutherford, NJ 07070
Ida Grae Products, 424 Laverne Ave., Mill Valley, CA 94941
Internatural Distributors, RFD Baker Hill Rd., Bradford, NJ 03221
Irma Shorell, Inc., 720 5th Ave., New York, NY 10019
Jason Natural Products, 8468 Warner Dr., Culver City, CA 90232
Jeanne Rose Herbal Body Works, 219 Carl St. A, San Francisco, CA 94117
JLM Enterprises, P.O. Box 593, Keego Harbor, MI 48033
Key West Fragrance and Cosmetic Factory, 524 Front St., Key West, FL 33041
Kimberly Sayer, Inc., 61 W. 82nd St. #5A, New York, NY 10024
Kiss My Face, P.O. Box 804, New Paltz, NY 12561
KMS, 6807 Highway E, Bella Vista, CA 96008
KSA Jojoba, 19025 Parthenia St. #200, Northridge, CA 91324
Lady Finelle, 137 Marston St., Lawrence, MA 01842
Laguna Soap Co., P.O. Box 6373, San Rafael, CA 94903
Levlad, Inc., 9183–5 Kelvin St., Chatsworth, CA 91311
Life Tree Products, 1448 12th St., Santa Monica, CA 90401
M&N Natural Products, P.O. Box 4502, Anaheim, CA 92803
Magic American Corp., 23700 Mercantile Rd., Beechwood, OH 44122–5955
Magic Lotion, 29002 N. Highway 1, Fort Bragg, CA 95437
Marly Savon Clair, P.O. Box 54841, Terminal Annex, Los Angeles, CA 90054
Martha Hill Cosmetics, Trudy Beaman, 5 Ivy Ct., Metuchen, NJ 08840
McGean–Rohco, Inc., 2910 Harvard Ave., Cleveland, OH 44109
Microbalanced Products, 25 Aladdin Ave., Dumont, NJ 07628
Mirror, Mirror on the Wall, 247 Everett St., Middleboro, MA 02346
Mountain Ocean Ltd., P.O. Box 951, Boulder, CO 80306
My Brother's Keeper, Inc., P.O. Box 1769, Richmond, IN 47375
Naturade, 7100 E. Jackson St., Paramount, CA 90723
Natural Organics, Inc., 10 Daniel St., Farmingdale, NY 11735
Nature Cosmetics, Inc., 881 Alma Real, Suite 101, Pacific Palisades, CA 90272
Nature de France, 145 Hudson St., New York, NY 10013
Nature's Colors, 424 Laverne Ave., Mill Valley, CA 94941
Nature's Gate Herbal Cosmetics, 9183–5 Kelvin St., Chatworth, CA 91311
Nelson Chemicals Co., 12345 Schaefer Hwy., Detroit, MI 48227

New World Minerals, 2880 N. Nellis Blvd., Las Vegas, NV 89110
Neway, 150 Causeway St., Boston, MA 02114
Nexxus, P.O. Box 4730, Santa Barbara, CA 93103
No Common Scents, King's Yard, Yellow Springs, OH 45387
North Country Soap, 7888 County Road #6, Maple Plain, MN 55359
Nutri–Metics International, Inc., 19501 E. Walnut Dr., City of Industry, CA 91748
O'Naturel, Inc., 535 Cordova Rd. #472, Santa Fe, NM 87501
Oriflame International, 76 Treble Cove Rd., N. Billerica, MA
Orjene Natural Cosmetics, 5–43 48th Ave., Long Island City, NY 11101
Patricia Allison Beauty Sorrority, P.O. Box 99968, San Diego, CA 92109
Paul Penders USA, P.O. Box 878, Seffner, FL 33584
Premier Industrial Corp., 4500 Euclid Ave., Cleveland, OH 44103
Professional and Technical Services Inc., 3333 NE Sandy Blvd. #208, Portland, OR 97232
Quintessence, 308 W. Lakeside St., Madison, WI 53715
Rainbow Research Corp., 170 Wilbur Place, Bohemia, NY 11716
WT Rawleigh Co., 223 E. Main St., Freeport, IL 61032
The Real Aloe Co., 4735–4D Industrial St., Simi Valley, CA 93063
Reviva Labs, Inc., 7–5 Hopkins Rd., Haddonfield, NJ 08033
Revlon, Inc., 767 5th Ave. New York, NY 10022
Rhizotome Co., P.O. Box 588, Boulder, CO 80306
Richlife, Inc., 2211 E. Orangewood, Anaheim, CA 92806–0240
I. Rokeach and Sons, Inc., 560 Sylvan Ave., Englewood Cliffs, NJ 07632
Schiff, 121 Moonachie Ave., Moonachie, NJ 07074
Shikai Products, P.O. Box 2866, Santa Rosa, CA 95405
Sirena Tropical Soap Co., P.O. Box 31673, Dallas, TX 75231
Solventol Chemical Products, Inc., 13177 Huron River Dr., Romulus, MI 48174
Sombra, 5600 G McLeod Ave., Albuquerque, NM 87109
Sparkle, AJ Funk & Co., 1471 Timber Dr., Elgin, IL 60120
St. Ives, Inc., 944 Indian Peak Rd., Rolling Hills, CA 90274
Sunrise Lane Products, Inc., 780 Greenwich St., New York, NY 10014
Sunshine Scented Oils, 1919 S. Burnside Ave., Los Angeles, CA 90016
Tom's of Maine, Railroad Ave., Kennebunk, ME 04042
Uncommon Scents, 1432 Williamette St., Eugene, OR 97401
Uni Pac Laboratory, 6355 N. Broadway, Chicago, IL 60660
Van Straaten Chemical Co., 630 W. Washington Blvd., Chicago, IL 60606
Vegan Street, P.O. Box 5525, Rockville, MD 20855
Velvet Products Co., P.O. Box 5459, Beverly Hills, CA 90210
Wala–Heilmittel, GmbH, Meadowbrook West, Wyoming, RI 02898
Warm Earth Cosmetics, 334 W. 19th St., Chico, CA 95928
Weleda, Inc., 841 S. Main St., Spring Valley, NY 10977

NOTE: SOME OF THESE COMPANIES USE ANIMAL BY-PRODUCTS. CHECK LABELS FOR
ANIMAL PRODUCTS SUCH AS **COLLAGEN, LANOLIN, HYDROLYZED ANIMAL
PROTEIN, KERATIN ETC.**

HUMANE MOUSETRAPS

Seabright, Ltd., 4026 Harlan St., Dept. 2, Emeryville, CA 94608

APPENDIX B
Statistics Concerning
Animal Agriculture and Meat Consumption

(Compiled from John Robbins' *Diet for A New America*, 1987, Frances Moore Lappé's *Diet for a Small Planet* and the Rainforest Action Network)

Environmental Statistics

•Historic cause of demise of many great civilizations: **Topsoil depletion**

•Percentage of original U.S. topsoil lost to date: **75%**

•Amount of U.S. cropland lost each year to soil erosion: **4 million acres (size of Connecticut)**

•Percentage of U.S. topsoil loss directly associated with livestock raising: **85%**

•Percentage of U.S. land area used for any type of agriculture: **52%**

•Percentage of U.S. agricultural land used for livestock production (including pasture, rangeland and cropland): **87%**

•Number of acres of U.S. forest which has been cleared to create cropland to produce a meat-centered diet: **260 million acres**

•How often an acre of U.S. trees disappears: **Every 8 seconds**

•Amount of trees spared per year by each individual who switches to a pure vegetarian* diet: **1 acre**

•Estimated rate of worldwide tropical rainforest deforestation per minute: **150 acres**

•Percentage of tropical rainforest deforestation directly linked with livestock raising: **50%**

•Year in which Central and South America will be stripped of tropical rainforest if present rate of deforestation occurs: **2010**

•Amount of meat imported annually by U.S. from Costa Rica, El Salvador, Guatemala, Nicaragua, Honduras and Panama: **200 million pounds**

•Amount of meat eaten by average person in Costa Rica, El Salvador, Guatemala, Nicaragua, Honduras and Panama: **Less than the average American house cat**

•Current rate of species extinction due to destruction of tropical rainforests and related habitats: **1,000/year**

•User of more than half of all water used for all purposes in the U.S.: **Livestock production**

•Water needed to produce 1 pound of wheat: **25 gallons**

•Water needed to produce 1 pound of meat: **2,500 gallons**

•Cost of hamburger meat if water used by meat industry was not subsidized by U.S. taxpayers: **$35/pound**

•Current cost for pound of protein from wheat: **$1.50**

•Current cost for pound of protein from beefsteak: **$15.40**

•Cost for pound of protein from beefsteak if U.S. taxpayers ceased subsidizing meat industry's use of water: **$89**

•Length of time world's petroleum reserves would last if all human beings ate a

meat-centered diet: **13 years**
- Length of time world's petroleum reserves would last if all human beings ate a vegetarian diet: **260 years**
- Barrels of oil imported daily by U.S.: **6,800,000 barrels**
- Percentage of energy return (as food energy per fossil energy expended) of *most energy-efficient* factory farming of meat: **34.5%**
- Percentage of energy return of *least energy-efficient* plant food: **328%**
- Pounds of soybeans produced by the amount of fossil fuel needed to produce 1 pound of feedlot beef: **40 pounds**
- Production of excrement by total U.S. human population:
12,000 pounds/second
- Production of excrement by U.S. livestock:
250,000 pounds/second
- Sewage systems in U.S. cities: **Common**
- Sewage systems in U.S. feedlots: **none**
- Amount of waste produced annually by U.S. livestock in confinement operations which is not recycled: **1 billion tons**
- Relative concentration of feedlot wastes compared to raw domestic sewage: **Ten to several hundred times more highly concentrated**
- Where feedlot waste often ends up: **In our water**

World Hunger Statistics

- Human population of the U.S.: **243 million**
- Number of humans who could be fed by the grain and soybeans eaten by U.S. livestock: **Over 1 billion**
- Percentage of corn grown in U.S. eaten by humans: **20%**
- Percentage of corn grown in U.S. eaten by livestock: **80%**
- Percentage of oats grown in U.S. eaten by livestock: **95%**
- Percentage of protein wasted by cycling grain through livestock: **90%**
- Percentage of carbohydrate wasted by cycling grain through livestock: **99%**
- Percentage of dietary fiber wasted by cycling grain through livestock: **100%**
- Pounds of potatoes that can be grown on 1 acre of land:
20,000 pounds
- Pounds of beef that can be produced on 1 acre of land: **165 pounds**
- Pounds of grain and soybeans needed to produce 1 pound
of feedlot beef: **16 pounds**
- Pounds of protein fed to chickens to produce 1 pound of protein as chicken flesh: **5 pounds**
- Pounds of protein fed to pigs to produce 1 pound of protein as pig flesh: **7.5 pounds**
- Number of pure vegetarians who can be fed on the amount of land needed to feed 1 person consuming a meat-centered diet: **20**
- How frequently a child dies of starvation: **Every 2 seconds**
- Number of children who starve to death every day: **40,000**
- Number of people who will starve to death this year: **60 million**

- Number of people who could be adequately fed by the grain saved if Americans reduced their intake of meat by 10%: **60 million**

Human Health Statistics

- Number of U.S. medical schools: **125**
- Number of U.S. medical schools with a required course in nutrition: **30**
- Training in nutrition received during 4 years of medical school by average U.S. physician: **2.5 hours**
- How frequently a heart attack strikes in U.S.: **Every 25 seconds**
- How frequently a heart attack kills in U.S.: **Every 45 seconds**
- Most common cause of death in U.S.: **Heart attack**
- Risk of death from heart attack by average American man: **50%**
- Risk of death from heart attack by average vegetarian* man: **15%**
- Risk of death from heart attack by average pure vegetarian man: **4%**
- Rise in blood cholesterol from consuming 1 egg per day: **12%**
- Rise in heart attack risk from 12% rise in blood cholesterol: **24%**
- Meat, dairy and egg industries claim there is no reason to be concerned about your blood cholesterol as long as it is: **"normal"**
- Your risk of dying of a disease caused by clogged arteries if your blood cholesterol is "normal:" **over 50%**
- Your risk of dying of a disease caused by clogged arteries if you do not consume saturated fat and cholesterol: **5%**
- Leading sources of saturated fat and cholesterol in American diets: **Meat, dairy products and eggs**
- Hollywood celebrity paid by Meat Board to tout beef as "Real food for real people:" **James Garner**
- Medical event experienced by James Garner in April, 1988: **Quintuple coronary artery bypass surgery**
- World populations with high meat intakes who do not have correspondingly high rates of colon cancer: **None**
- World populations with low meat intakes who do not have correspondingly low rates of colon cancer: **None**
- Increased risk of breast cancer for women who eat meat daily compared to women who eat meat less than once a week: **4 times higher**
- Increased risk of fatal ovarian cancer for women who eat eggs 3 or more times a week compared to women who eat eggs less than once a week: **3 times higher**
- Foods men in U.S. are conditioned to think of as "manly:" **Animal products**
- Increased risk of fatal prostate cancer for men who consume meats, cheese, eggs and milk daily compared to men who eat these foods sparingly or not at all: **3.6 times higher**
- The meat, dairy and egg industries tell us: animal products constitute 2 of the "Basic 4" food groups
- The meat, dairy and egg industries don't tell us: **There were originally 12 official basic food groups before these industries applied enormous pressure on behalf of their products**
- The meat, dairy and egg industries tell us: **We are well-fed only with animal products**

- The meat, dairy and egg industries don't tell us: The diseases which are commonly prevented, consistently improved, and sometimes cured by a low-fat, vegetarian diet include:

strokes, heart disease, osteoporosis, kidney stones, breast cancer, colon cancer, prostate cancer, pancreatic cancer, ovarian cancer, cervical cancer, stomach cancer, endometrial cancer, diabetes, hypoglycemia, kidney disease, peptic ulcers, constipation, hemorrhoids, hiatal hernias, diverticulosis, obesity, gallstones, hypertension, asthma, salmonellosis, trichinosis, irritable colon syndrome

- Pesticide residues in U.S. diet supplied by meat: **55%**
- Pesticide residues in U.S. diet supplied by dairy products: **23%**
- Pesticide residues in U.S. diet supplied by vegetables: **6%**
- Pesticide residues in U.S. diet supplied by fruits: **4%**
- Pesticide residues in U.S. diet supplied by grains: **1%**
- Percentage of U.S. mother's milk containing significant levels of DDT: **99%**
- Percentage of U.S. vegetarian mother's milk containing significant levels of DDT: **8%**
- Percentage of male college students sterile in 1950: **.5%**
- Percentage of male college students sterile in 1978: **25%**
- Sperm count of average American male compared to 30 years ago: **Down 30%**
- Principal reason for sterility and sperm count reduction in U.S. men: **Chlorinated hydrocarbon pesticides (including DDT, dioxin, etc.)**
- Percentage of chlorinated hydrocarbon pesticide residues in American diet attributable to meats, dairy products, fish and eggs: **94%**
- The United States Department of Agriculture (USDA) tells us: **Our meat is inspected**
- The USDA doesn't tell us: **Less than 1 out of every quarter million slaughtered animals is tested for toxic chemical residues**
- Percentage of total antibiotics used in U.S. fed routinely to livestock: **55%**
- Percentage of staphylococci infections resistant to penicillin in 1960: **13%**
- Percentage of staphylococci infections resistant to penicillin in 1988: **91%**
- Reason: **Breeding of antibiotic resistant bacteria in factory farms due to routine feeding of antibiotics to livestock**
- Effectiveness of all antibiotics: **Declining rapidly**
- Reason: **Breeding of antibiotic-resistant bacteria in factory farms due to routine feeding of antibiotics to livestock**
- Response by entire European Economic Community to routine feeding of antibiotics to livestock: **Ban**
- Response by American meat and pharmaceutical industries to routine feeding of antibiotics to livestock:
Full and complete support

A pure vegetarian (known as a vegan) is an individual who consumes no animal products at all. A vegetarian is an individual who consumes no animal flesh, but who may consume dairy products and/or eggs.

APPENDIX C
Tips for Screening Animal Adoption Calls

Every time people advertise animals as available for adoption, there is a very real danger that they may hand over their animals to dealers, occultists, or irresponsible pet owners.

Laboratory animal dealers and occult practitioners are actively pursuing animals advertised in the classified section of the newspaper. Occultists often inquire about black kittens, white kittens and black and white kittens, in that order. Sometimes they will settle for adult cats of the same colors. Some sects kill German Shepherd dogs, which places these animals at risk.

Animal fighting enthusiasts pose an additional concern, because they often contact advertisers with the aim of collecting smaller animals to sacrifice in the training of their violent dogs.

Be aware that dealers and occultists can be shrewd and dishonest. They will tell you what you want to hear and make serious efforts to disguise their true motives. (e.g. "I had a dog just like that for sixteen years, and she just died of cancer." "My daughter is going to be so pleased that I found a dog like Fido for her." "I love black cats, and I don't understand why so many people are afraid of them.")

The following suggestions should help you avoid handing an animal over to an uncertain or unpleasant fate:

• Be sure that you want to place the animal outside of your home. Are there any behavioral or physical problems with the animal that are causing you specific difficulties? It is possible that these could be addressed with the help of an SPCA staff member, a professional trainer, or a veterinarian. These problems are often easier to solve than you might imagine.

• If you are trying to place a young puppy, make sure that the potential adoptor is prepared to be at home regularly with the animal. No puppy should be left at home all day while the owner is at work or school.

• Ask for the name, telephone number and address of the caller so that you can verify the information which you are given in the telephone book or through directory assistance. Dealers usually will not be willing to show or to provide proof of identity or to offer correct names and addresses.

• Determine whether the caller lives in a rented or owned home. If the caller rents, contact the landlord, landlady or management to verify that animals are permitted in the building.

• Ask for personal references, particularly from neighbors. A legitimate caller will not begrudge this information since she or he will know that the request stems from a sincere desire to provide the animal with a good home.

• Ask the caller for a veterinary reference. By contacting the caller's veterinarian, you can find out whether former or other animals owned by the caller have received necessary vaccinations and other health care.

• Request a visit to the potential adoptor's home so that you can see for yourself the conditions under which the animal will live.

• Tell the caller that you would like to have his or her guarantee that you will be contacted if things are not working out with the animal. Some people do not show much patience about housebreaking or behavioral problems. By insisting that you be contacted as a first option should any difficulties arise, you can ensure that you will have another chance to find the animal a suitable home.

• Ask the caller if her or his yard is fenced in or well-suited for an animal, or if she or he has small children who may need to be given instruction about responsible pet care.

• For dogs, find out whether the caller plans to keep the animal outside all the time. Dogs are social animals and should be part of the family. If the caller plans to let the dog live outside, even in an insulated dog house, do not release the animal to him or her.

QUESTIONS WHICH YOU SHOULD ASK POTENTIAL ADOPTORS:

• Do you plan to spay or neuter this animal when he or she reaches reproductive maturity? (If the answer is no, don't release your animal to them. Millions of animals are killed in the nation's pounds and shelters every year because there are not enough homes. It is irresponsible to contribute to this tragedy by giving animals to people who might let them reproduce.)

• Have you had pets before? What happened to them? (If the animals were given away, lost, etc., don't release your animal to the caller unless you are certain that his or her animal care habits have changed.)

• What will you do with the animal in the event that you have to relocate to another area? (Unless the caller would plan on keeping the animal in such a case, think twice about releasing the animal to her or him.)

• What is your interest in looking for a companion animal at this time? Are you doing so for companionship? For love? Because you love animals? (These are good reasons. If the caller wants a dog to protect the house or a cat to catch mice, BEWARE!)

Remember: While you may feel that it is impolite to ask probing questions, the animal's life may be at risk, and you are ultimately responsible for the well-being of any animal you give away.

APPENDIX D
Organizations to Contact
for Further Information

PRO-ANIMAL PROTECTION, RIGHTS AND/OR WELFARE

MULTI-ISSUE

American Humane Association
(AHA)
63 Inverness Drive East
Englewood, CO 80112

American Society for the Prevention
of Cruelty to Animals (ASPCA)
441 E. 92nd St.
New York, NY 10128

Animal Protection Institute (API)
P.O. Box 22505
Sacramento, CA 95822

Animal Rights Coalition (ARC)
P.O. Box 20315
Bloomington, MN 55420

Animal Welfare Institute (AWI)
P.O. Box 3650
Washington, DC 20007

Argus Archives
228 E. 49th St.
New York, NY 10017

Animal Rights Mobilization (ARM!)
P.O. Box 1553
Williamsport, PA 17703

Citizens to End Animal Suffering
and Exploitation (CEASE)
P.O. Box 27
Cambridge, MA 02238

Culture and Animals Foundation
(CAF)
3509 Eden Croft Drive
Raleigh, NC 27612

Earthsave Foundation
P.O. Box 949
Felton, CA 98018-0949

Feminists for Animal Rights
P.O. Box 10017
Berkeley, CA 94709

Friends of Animals (FoA)
P.O. Box 1244
Norwalk, CT 06856

The Fund for Animals
200 W. 57th St.
New York, NY 10019

Humane Society of the United States
(HSUS)
2100 L St. NW
Washington, DC 20037

International Fund for Animal Welfare
(IFAW)
P.O. Box 193
Yarmouth port, MA 02675

International Society for
Animal Rights (ISAR)
421 South State Street
Clarks Summit, PA 18411

People for the Ethical Treatment
of Animals (PETA)
P.O. Box 42516
Washington, DC 20015

Progressive Animal Welfare Society
(PAWS)
P.O. Box 1037
Lynnwood, WA 98046

LAB ANIMAL PROTECTION AND/OR ANTI-VIVISECTION

American Anti-Vivisection Society (AA-VS)
Suite 204 Noble Plaza
801 Old York Rd.
Jenkintown, PA 19046

American Fund for Alternatives to Animal Research (AFAAR)
175 W. 12th St. Suite 16G
New York, NY 10011

Animal Rights International
P.O. Box 214, Planetarium Station
New York, NY 10024

Committee for Responsible Research
P.O. Box 1626
Cambridge, MA 02238

Disabled and Incurably Ill for Alternatives to Animal Research (DIIAAR)
1733 Grant Street #F
Berkeley, CA 94703

In Defense of Animals (IDA)
816 West Francisco Blvd.
San Rafael, CA 94901

Last Chance for Animals (LCA)
18653 Ventura Blvd. #356
Tarzana, CA 91356

National Anti-Vivisection Society (NAVS)
53 West Jackson Blvd. Suite 1550
Chicago, IL 60604

New England Anti-Vivisection Society (NEAVS)
333 Washington St. #850
Boston, MA 02108

S.U.P.R.E.S.S.
P.O. Box 1062
Pasadena, CA 91102

United Action for Animals (UAA)
205 E. 42nd St.
New York, NY 10017

PROFESSIONAL ORGANIZATIONS

Association of Veterinarians for Animal Rights (AVAR)
P.O. Box 6269
Vacaville, CA 95696

Medical Research and Modernization Committee (MRMC)
P.O. Box 6036 Grand Central Station
New York, NY 10163-6018

National Association of Nurses Against Vivisection (NANAV)
P.O. Box 42110
Washington, DC 20015

Physicians Committee for Responsible Medicine (PCRM)
P.O. Box 6322
Washington, DC 20015

Psychologists for the Ethical Treatment of Animals (PsyETA)
P.O. Box 87
New Gloucester, ME 04260

STUDENT AND HUMANE EDUCATION ORGANIZATIONS

Animalearn
Suite 204 Noble Plaza
801 Old York Road
Jenkintown, PA 19046

Humane Education Committee (HEC)
P.O. Box 445
New York, NY 10128

National Association for Humane and Environmental Education
(NAHEE)
P.O. Box 362
East Haddam, CT 06423
(Humane Education publications)

Student Action Corps for Animals
(SACA)
P.O. Box 15588
Washington, DC 20003-0588

FOOD ANIMAL ISSUES

Food Animal Concerns Trust (FACT)
P.O. Box 14599
Chicago, IL 60614

Farm Animal Reform Movement
(FARM)
P.O. Box 70123
Washington, DC 20088

Farm Sanctuary
P.O. Box 150
Watkins Glen, NY 14891

Humane Farming Association (HFA)
1550 California St.
San Francisco, CA 94109

HUNTING

Committee to Abolish Sport Hunting
(CASH)
P.O. Box 43
White Plains, NY 10605

The Fund for Animals
850 Sligo Ave. Suite LL2
Silver Spring, MD 20910

WILDLIFE ISSUES

Alaska Wildlife Alliance
P.O. Box 190953
Anchorage, AK 99519

American Endangered Species
Foundation
1988 Damascus Rd. Rt. 4
Golden, CO 80403

Defenders of Wildlife
1244 19th St. NW
Washington, DC 20036

PRIMATES

International Primate Protection
League (IPPL)
P.O. Box 766
Summerville, SC 29484

Primarily Primates
P.O. Box 15306
San Antonio, TX 78212-8506

POLITICAL, LEGISLATIVE AND LEGAL ORGANIZATIONS

Animal Legal Defense Fund (ALDF)
1363 Lincoln Ave.
San Rafael, CA 94901

National Alliance for Animals
P.O. Box 2978
Washington, DC 20013

Rutgers Animal Rights Law Clinic
Rutgers University College of Law
15 Washington St.
Newark, NJ 07102-3192

MARINE ANIMAL AND ENVIRON-MENTAL ORGANIZATIONS

Earth Island Institute
300 Broadway Suite 28
San Francisco, CA 94133

Greenpeace
1611 Connecticut Ave. NW
Washington, DC 20009

Sea Shepherd Conservation Society
P.O. Box 7000S
Redondo Beach, CA 90277

MEDIA

Animal Rights Information Service
(ARIS)
P.O. Box 20671, Columbus Circle
New York, NY 10023

Focus on Animals
P.O. Box 150
Trumbull, CT 06611

Gaia Institute
P.O. Box 852
South Lynnfield, MA 01940

PUBLICATIONS

The Animals' Agenda
456 Monroe Turnpike
Monroe, CT 06468

The Animals' Voice Magazine
P.O. Box 341347
Los Angeles, CA 90034

Between the Species
P.O. Box 254
Berkeley, CA 94701

FOREIGN ORGANIZATIONS

Australia

Animal Liberation
P.O. Box 15, Elmwood
Victoria

Canada

Animal Liberation Collective
CP 148, S. Durham
Quebec, JOH 2CO

Association Ahimsa
Ste-Rita
Quebec GOL 4G0

Animal Alliance of Canada
1640 Bayview Ave. #1016
Toronto, Ontario M4G 4E9

Lifeforce Foundation
P.O. Box 3117 Main post Office
Vancouver, V6B 3X6

United Kingdom

Advocates for Animals
10 Queensferry St.
Edinburgh, EH2 4PG Scotland

Animal Aid
7 Castle Street
Tonbridge, Kent
TN9 1BH England

Animal Concern
62 Old Dumbarton Rd.
Glasgow G3 8RG Scotland

British Union for the Abolition of
Vivisection (BUAV)
16a Crane Grove
London N7 8LB England

Compassion in World Farming (CIWF)
20 Lavant St. Petersfield
Hampshire GU32 3EW England

Irish Anti-Vivisection Society
P.O. Box 13
Greystones
Co. Wicklow, Ireland

National Anti-Vivisection Society
(NAVS)
83 Upper Rd.
Kennington, Oxford OX1 5LW
England

Royal Society for the Prevention of
Cruelty to Animals (RSPCA)
Causeway Horsham, Sussex
England

International

International Association Against
Painful Experiments on Animals
(IAAPEA)
P.O. Box 215 St. Albans
Herts AL3 4RD England

World Society for the Protection of
Animals (WSPA)
29 Perkins St.
Boston, MA 02130

PRO-ANIMAL USE

PRO FUR, HUNTING & TRAPPING

The American Fur Industry
101 W. 30th St.
New York, NY

Fur Farm Animal Welfare Coalition
405 Sidley St. Suite 120
St. Paul, MN 55101

Fur Information Council of America
(FICA)
655 15th St. NW
Washington, DC 20005

National Rifle Association (NRA)
1600 Rhode Island Ave. NW
Washington, DC 20036
National Trappers Association (NTA)
P.O. Box 3667
Bloomington, IL 61701

National Wildlife Federation (NWF)
1412 16th St. NW
Washington, DC 20036
(publications)

PRO VIVISECTION

American Medical Association (AMA)
535 N. Dearborn St.
Chicago, IL 60610

American Psychological Association
(APA)
1200 17th St. NW
Washington, DC 20036

American Veterinary Medical
Association (AVMA)
930 N. Meacham Rd.
Schaumburg, IL 60196

Foundation for Biomedical Research
(FBR)
818 Connecticut Ave. Suite 303 NW
Washington, DC 20006

(publications)
Incurably Ill For Animal Research
(iiFAR)
P.O. Box 1873
Bridgeview, IL 60455

PRO INTENSIVE ANIMAL AGRICULTURE

American Egg Board
1460 Renaissance Dr.
Park Ridge, IL 60068

American Meat Institute (AMI)
1700 N. Moore St.
Arlington, VA 22209

American Veal Association (AVA)
1804 Naper Blvd. #241
Naperville, IL 60563
Farm Animal Welfare Council (FAWC)
600 Maryland Ave. SW
Washington, DC 20024

National Broiler Council (NBC)
1155 15th St. NW
Washington, DC 20005

National Cattlemen's Association
(NCA)
1301 Pennsylvania Ave. NW
Washington, DC 20004

National Dairy Council (NDC)
6300 N. River Rd.
Rosemont, IL 60018

United Egg Producers
3951 Snapfinger Parkway
Decatur, GA 30035

Veal Industry Council
P.O. Box 587139
Chicago, IL 60658

APPENDIX E
Alternatives to Dissection

Alternatives Hotline: 800-922-FROG

This hotline is staffed by Pat Graham whose daughter, Jenifer, successfully fought for her right to refuse dissection in California. The hotline was developed to provide advice and alternatives for students around the country who do not wish to dissect animals. The hotline also helps students to approach teachers and administrators effectively.

Computer Programs

The Human Body: An Overview: Cambridge Development Laboratory, Inc., 214 Third Ave., Waltham, MA 02154, 800-637-0047, MA: 617-890-4640. Apple, junior high.

This program teaches students to identify the six major physiological systems: muscular, digestive, respiratory, circulatory, nervous and skeletal. The program includes animated graphs.

The Probe Series: Cambridge Development Laboratory, Inc., 214 Third Ave., Waltham, MA 02154, 800-637-0047, MA: 617-890-4640, Apple, junior high to high school.

The Probe Series includes 22 computer programs that allow the student to focus on particular organs. The Heart Probe has an animated heartbeat which demonstrates the interactions of all four valves. Blood flow is distinguished by its change of color when it flows to and from the heart. In the Brain Probe, the student moves the indicator to an area of the brain, and prompts the computer to identify and define the structure at hand. The program explores the brain in three different sections: the saggital midsection, the frontal midsection, and the cerebral cortex.

Visifrog: Carolina Biological Supply Company, 2700 York Rd., Burlington, SC 27215, 800-334-5551, junior high to high school.

Visifrog is a computer program that uses high-resolution color graphics to explore the anatomical structures of a frog. The program includes an identification game, a data retrieval, and a quiz. In the identification game, the indicator points to an anatomical structure on the frog, and the student keys in the correct answer. The data retrieval system is a visual database of anatomical structures and functions by calling up a description when the student points to a particular structure.

Slides

An Introduction to Human Anatomy: Wards Biological Supply Company, P.O. Box 92912, 5100 W. Henrietta Rd., Rochester, NY 14692-9012, 800-962-2660, high school and beyond.

An Introduction to Human Anatomy contains a series of slides, taken by a practicing pathologist, depicting both normal and diseased conditions. An informative text accompanies the slides. The series includes the following systems: cardiovascular, respiratory, hematopoietic, gastrointestinal, hepatobiliary, endocrine, urinary, nervous, skeletal and reproductive.

Videotapes and Videodiscs

The Body in Focus: Cambridge Development Laboratory, Inc., 214 Third Ave., Waltham, MA 02154, 800-637-0047, MA: 617-890-4640. Apple, grades 5-11.

This video allows students to observe interesting mechanisms such as the opening and closing of the vocal chords in response to sneezing, and the manner in which the biceps and triceps work. Students can also dissect the head, arm and torso through the program. The program also includes a game which tests the knowledge students have gained.

The Human Anatomy Series: Teaching Films, Inc., 930 Pitner Ave., Evanston, IL 60202, 800-323-9084, high school and beyond.

The Human Anatomy Series presents videos of different regions of the body - upper extremity, thorax, abdomen and pelvis, lower extremity, neuroanatomy, and head and neck. Each region is demonstrated with the use of live models, specimens, x-rays and graphics.

The Heart Simulator, The Digestion Simulator, The Kidney: Structure and Function: Cambridge Development Laboratory, Inc., 214 Third Ave., Waltham, MA 02154, 800-637-0047, MA: 617-890-4640. Apple, junior high to high school.

These videos demonstrate the various systems in the human body. *The Kidney* is more advanced than the other simulations.

Your Body: Series I, II, and III: Cambridge Development Laboratory, Inc., 214 Third Ave., Waltham, MA 02154, 800-637-0047, MA: 617-890-4640. Grades 6-12.

This series of videos teaches students the roles of bones, muscles, tissues, organs and whole systems in a fairly simplified manner.

The Living Body: Films for the Humanities and Sciences, P.O. Box 2053, Princeton, NJ, 800-257-5126, NJ: 609-452-1128, high school and beyond.

The Living Body consists of 26 videotapes that describe virtually every function of the human body from the senses to cell duplication to muscle power. The films take the viewer inside the body to watch how the systems function and interact.

It's a Frog's Life: Carolina Biological Supply Company, Burlington 2700 York Rd., Burlington, NC 27215, 800-334-5551, junior high to high school.

This video describes a wide range of adaptations that allow different species of frogs to survive.

Books and Charts

The Endangered Species Handbook: The Animal Welfare Institute, P.O. Box 3650, Washington, DC 20007, 202-337-2332, all ages.

This excellent handbook is available free to teachers. All aspects of the endangered species dilemma are covered, from causes and consequences of vanishing wildlife to legislation and citizen action. The handbook includes a number of suggestions for humane biology projects.

The Anatomy Coloring Book: Wards Biological Supply Company, P.O. Box 92912, 5100 W. Henrietta Rd., Rochester, NY 14692-9012, 800-962-2660, fifth grade and beyond.

The Anatomy Coloring Book teaches structures and concepts through the process of coloring. There are 142 plates and all are cross referenced. The book begins with the single cell and gradually moves up to separate systems.

The Human Anatomy Series Charts: Denoyer-Geppert Science Co., 5215-5225 N. Ravenswood Ave., Chicago, IL 60640, 800-621-1014, fifth grade and beyond.

These classroom charts measure 44" x 66" and are fully detailed and printed in color. Each includes cross-sections and macroscopic views of different areas of the body.

Physiological Studies

Intelitool: Intelitool, P.O. Box 459, Batavia, Il 60510-0459, 800-227-3805, IL: 312-406-1041, high school and beyond.

Students participate in actual ECG's, biofeedback, motor point stimulation, single muscle twitch, and many other activities designed to teach physiological concepts.

The Bio-Meter: Phipps and Bird, Inc., 8741 Landmark Rd., Box 27324, Richmond, VA 23261, 804-264-7590, high school and beyond.

The Bio-Meter is a small, inexpensive, battery-operated device which studies heart function. Students are able to study their own hearts. Variability between sexes, athletes, smokers etc. can be compared.

Biofeedback Microlab: Cambridge Development Laboratory, Inc., 214 Third Ave., Waltham, MA 02154, 800-637-0047, MA: 617-890-4640, high school and beyond.

Students can measure pulse rate, galvanic skin response, electromyograph and skin temperature. Using sensitive instrumentation, students learn to control various physiological reactions.

Cell Biology

Cellserv: The Center for Advanced Training in Cell and Molecular Biology (CATCMB), 103 McCort-Ward Bldg., Catholic University, Washington, DC 20064, 202-635-5276, high school.

Cellserv, funded by the American Fund for Alternatives to Animal Research, provides high school biology classes with fixed cell cultures. The materials are supplemented by detailed instructions, background information and videos.

Non-Animal Methods Handbooks

Alternatives in Biology Education NEAVS, 333 Washington St., Boston, MA 12108, (617) 523-2237, junior high and high school.

This booklet lists alternatives to dissection. While comprehensive, this booklet does list videos and other materials which have relied upon actual dissection.

Alternatives to Dissection National Association for Humane and Environmental Education (NAHEE), 67 Salem Road, E. Haddam, CT 06423, junior high and high school.

This manual contains a variety of well-constructed lesson plans and activities, and provides several pages of resource materials including useful catalogues.

Animal Alternatives Handbook SACA, P.O. Box 15588, Washington, DC 20003, (202) 543-8983, junior high and high school.

This booklet lists alternatives to dissection. Unlike some other handbooks, none of the suggestions or materials listed in this manual rely on animals.

The Responsible Use of Animals in the Classroom: Including Alternatives to Dissection National Association of Biology Teachers, 11250 Roger Bacon Dr. #19, Reston, VA 22090, junior high and high school.

This book, published by the National Association of Biology Teachers, includes several useful exercises and lesson plans, although there are several activities which do utilize animals.

Other Possibilities

1. Study animals in their natural environments through careful observation.

2. Obtain permission to observe procedures at a veterinary or human hospital.

APPENDIX F
Evaluating a Zoo

When visiting a zoo, observe animals with a critical eye. Using the following guidelines, evaluate the conditions for the animals. You may want to follow up your visit by writing to the director or curator of the zoo with your comments.

1. Are animals confined in areas which resemble their natural habitats and which provide for species specific stimulation?

2. Are social animals confined alone or in groups?

3. Are animals pacing aimlessly, rocking back and forth, plucking their feathers, chewing on their bodies, or exhibiting any other neurotic behaviors attributable to stress or boredom?

4. Are cages clean, free from feces, urine and old food?

5. Do animals appear healthy, neither too fat nor too skinny, with bright eyes (except for molting reptiles) and without sores?

6. Are there many newborns? Ask zoo officials about the plans for the newborns as they mature.

7. Are playful animals provided with toys or other objects for amusement?

8. Can animals escape the stares and taunts of human visitors, or are the animals constantly on display?

9. Are nocturnal animals in darkened, soundproof quarters, or are they subject to human disturbance during the day?

10. Are birds able to fly, or have their wings been clipped? Are birds in cages which are large enough for flight? Do they have several perches and hiding areas?

11. Is temperature regulated appropriately for different animal species?

12. Are marine mammals kept in groups in clean tanks or are animals isolated in small pools? Do the tanks have chlorine or other chemicals in them which irritate the animals' eyes? Check with the marine mammal specialist to ascertain the longevity of the animals in captivity. How does their longevity in captivity compare to their longevity in the wild?

13. Are animals who normally burrow or dig housed on concrete which prevents burrowing, or are they provided with burrows, soil, and other opportunities to dig?

14. Are the great apes housed in social groups, with toys, climbing facilities, hiding areas and bedding materials?

15. Are keepers nearby to monitor visitor and animal behavior and interaction?

16. Are animals chained or free in large areas?

17. Have you read about accidents at the zoo? Has the zoo corrected problems?

18. Does the zoo have a petting animal exhibit? Are children given instruction about how to pet animals before entering the pens? Do the animals have a place to hide or a way to get away from the children?

[For more information about evaluating a zoo, contact Zoo Check, Cherry Tree Cottage, Coldharbour, Nr. Dorking, Surrey RH5 6HA, England]

APPENDIX G
Getting Involved
Students with an interest in animal protection
may find the following activities useful:

Writing to legislators

You may want to write to your Senators, Representatives, and other elected officials to express your opinions. Your representatives in the legislative and executive departments of local, state and federal government exist to serve you. You may want to write to urge them to support or oppose legislation, to request them to sponsor or even initiate legislation, or to send you a copy of legislation already initiated. To find out the names, addresses and phone numbers of your elected officials, call the League of Women Voters. You can find the League's number in the telephone directory. For federal legislators and other government officials, the following addresses may be useful:

Senator

The Honorable _____

United States Senate

Washington, DC 20510

Representative

The Honorable _____

House of Representatives

Washington, DC 20515

President

The President

The White House

Washington, DC 20500

Vice-President

The Vice-President

The White House

Washington, DC 20500

Member of the Cabinet

The Honorable _____

The Secretary of _____

Washington, DC 20210

Boycotting Companies
and Writing to Company Directors

You may want to boycott products produced by companies which perform animal tests, pollute the planet, or otherwise cause harm to animals or the environment. You can write to the Chief Executive Officers (CEO's) of each company explaining why you and your family will no longer purchase their products. To obtain the address of a company scrutinize the packaging of the product; the company name and address will likely be on the container. You can also consult the Standard and Poors Corporate Records at your local library for company addresses.

Leafletting and Tabling

Together with several friends you can quite easily distribute flyers in a public place. You can obtain bulk quantities of flyers from most animal protection organizations. Your leafletting may be seasonal (e.g. distributing flyers about fur coats in winter) or focused around an event (e.g. leafletting when the circus comes to town). You may also want to get involved with local grassroots organizations and volunteer to staff a table at a mall or town event. Remember to check with local police to find out the laws regarding distribution of literature in public places.

Non-violent Protesting

By contacting animal organizations in your area and requesting that they inform you of local activities, you can get involved with non-violent protests concerning animal suffering. For example, many grassroots organizations stage protests against particularly cruel and unnecessary animal experiments during "World Laboratory Animal Liberation Week" at the end of April, against factory farming on March 20, The Great American Meatout, and during hunting season. Demonstrations and protests are effective at alerting companies, government and the media to public concerns. They also provide the motivation for government and corporate officials to initiate changes to alleviate animal suffering.

School Activities

You may want to start an animal advocacy group at school under the sponsorship of a sympathetic teacher. With an active school group you can help animals significantly. You can:

•Organize an animal awareness day in school.

•Invite speakers to give presentations on animal issues at assemblies or for interested students.

•Arrange a debate between those who support and those who oppose animal use.

•Set up an information table in a good location from time to time.

•Work with classmates, teachers and school administrators on recycling issues: schools can purchase recycled paper as well as recycle waste paper, cans, bottles and other materials.

•Emphasize the connections between animal protection issues and other issues such as environmental, health, peace and world hunger concerns.

•Work with teachers, administrators and other students to obtain a school policy regarding dissection.

•Ask the school to serve nutritious vegetarian lunches.

•Organize an animal care group at school to monitor the care of classroom pets.

•Monitor projects which use animals, such as 4-H chick-hatching activities.

•Sponsor fundraising events to raise money for animal protection and environmental activities.

INDEX

Zoe Weil is a professional environmental and animal issues educator. She earned Masters degrees from the University of Pennsylvania and Harvard Divinity School. She has worked for many years as a humane educator, naturalist and wildlife rehabilitator. Zoe lives with two dogs, four cats and a spouse.